children's party
cakes & cookies

children's party cakes & cookies

A mouthwatering selection of more than
180 recipes for novelty cakes, cookies, buns
and muffins for kids' parties

More than 200 beautiful photographs
with step-by-step instructions

Editor: Martha Day

southwater

This edition is published by Southwater, an imprint of
Anness Publishing Ltd, Hermes House, 88–89 Blackfriars Road,
London SE1 8HA; tel. 020 7401 2077; fax 020 7633 9499

www.southwaterbooks.com; www.annesspublishing.com

If you like the images in this book and would like to investigate using
them for publishing, promotions or advertising, please visit our website
www.practicalpictures.com for more information.

UK agent: The Manning Partnership Ltd; tel. 01225 478444;
fax 01225 478440; sales@manning-partnership.co.uk
UK distributor: Grantham Book Services Ltd; tel. 01476 541080;
fax 01476 541061; orders@gbs.tbs-ltd.co.uk
North American agent/distributor: National Book Network;
tel. 301 459 3366; fax 301 429 5746; www.nbnbooks.com
Australian agent/distributor: Pan Macmillan Australia;
tel. 1300 135 113; fax 1300 135 103;
customer.service@macmillan.com.au
New Zealand agent/distributor: David Bateman Ltd;
tel. (09) 415 7664; fax (09) 415 8892

Publisher: Joanna Lorenz
Senior Managing Editor: Conor Kilgallon
Editors: Lucy Doncaster and Liz Woodland
Copy Editor: Jan Cutler
Design: SMI
Photographers: Karl Adamson, Edward Allwright, David Armstrong,
Steve Baxter, James Duncan, John Freeman, Michelle Garrett, Amanda
Heywood, Tim Hill, Don Last, Michael Michaels
Recipes: Alex Barker, Carole Clements, Roz Denny, Christine France,
Shirley Gill, Patricia Lousada, Norma MacMillan, Sue Maggs, Janice Murfitt,
Annie Nichols, Louise Pickford, Katherine Richmond, Hilaire Walden,
Steven Wheeler, Elizabeth Wolf-Cohen
Food for Photography: Carla Capalbo, Carole Handslip, Wendy Lee,
Sarah Maxwell, Angela Nilsen, Jane Stevenson, Liz Trigg, Elizabeth
Wolf-Cohen
Stylists: Madeleine Brehaut, Maria Kelly, Blake Minton, Kirsty Rawlings,
Fiona Tillett
Editorial Reader: Rosie Fairhead
Production Controller: Pedro Nelson

Previously published as part of a larger volume, *500 Cakes and Bakes*.

Main front cover image shows Ladybird Cake – for recipe, see page 53

Ethical Trading Policy
Because of our ongoing ecological investment programme, you, as our
customer, can have the pleasure and reassurance of knowing that a tree
is being cultivated on your behalf to naturally replace the materials used
to make the book you are holding. For further information about this
scheme, go to www.annesspublishing.com/trees

Notes
Bracketed terms are intended for American readers.
For all recipes, quantities are given in both metric and imperial measures
and, where appropriate, in standard cups and spoons. Follow one set of
measures, but not a mixture, because they are not interchangeable.
Standard spoon and cup measures are level.
1 tsp = 5ml, 1 tbsp = 15ml, 1 cup = 250ml/8fl oz.
Australian standard tablespoons are 20ml. Australian readers should
use 3 tsp in place of 1 tbsp for measuring small quantities.
American pints are 16fl oz/2 cups. American readers should use
20fl oz/2.5 cups in place of 1 pint when measuring liquids.
Electric oven temperatures in this book are for conventional ovens.
When using a fan oven, the temperature will probably need to be
reduced by about 10–20°C/20–40°F. Since ovens vary, you should
check with your manufacturer's instruction book for guidance.
The nutritional analysis given for each recipe is calculated per serving
or item, unless otherwise stated. If the recipe gives a range, such as
Serves 4–6, then the nutritional analysis will be for the smaller portion
size, i.e. 6 servings. Measurements for sodium do not include salt
added to taste.
Medium (US large) eggs are used unless otherwise stated.

Contents

Introduction

Aspecial cake is the perfect way to celebrate a child's birthday or any other important event, and can be specifically designed with the interests of the child in mind.

This fabulous recipe book is packed full of ideas for fun and fantasy cakes for children of all ages, that can be achieved with ease – each recipe is illustrated by a beautiful colour photograph of the finished product, and the step-by-step instructions are so simple and straightforward that even a beginner will find them easy to follow.

The chapters range from cookies and bars, which include delights such as Chunky Chocolate Drops and Peanut Butter Cookies, to simple teatime cakes, such as One-Stage Victoria Sponge and Fairy Cakes. You will also find elaborate ideas for novelty cakes for birthdays and special celebrations which will delight any child – try an exquisite Fairy Castle Cake or a Racing Ring Cake.

Cake decorating does not have to be as time-consuming as the results might suggest. In this book there are plenty of decorating ideas that can be achieved with mininum fuss and with maximum child appeal, using candies, chocolates, and coloured frostings. Beginners will find it easy to create professional-looking fun cakes, while more advanced cooks will be inspired by the wide range of delightful ideas illustrated within.

In fact, novice cooks often make the best bakers, preheating the oven in plenty of time, taking care to measure ingredients accurately and following recipe methods to the letter. All of these elements are important in baking, which demands more precision than many other types of cooking. It is well worth reading the chosen recipe carefully before you begin baking, as well as doing any preparation, such as browning almonds or softening butter, in advance, then setting out the measured ingredients in the style of the TV cook.

In this book you will find everything you need to make your child's party a success, from savoury Cheese Bread to American Chocolate Fudge Brownies, and a whole range of cakes representing animals, clowns and many other fun ideas – there's sure to be one that will just hit the spot.

Meringues

You can make these classic meringues as large or small as you like.

Makes about 24 small meringues
4 egg whites
1.5ml/¼ tsp salt

275g/10oz/scant 1¼ cups caster (superfine) sugar
2.5ml/½ tsp vanilla or almond extract (optional)

To serve
250ml/8fl oz/1 cup whipping cream

1 Preheat the oven to 110°C/225°F/Gas ¼. Grease and flour two large baking sheets.

2 Beat the egg whites and salt in a metal bowl. When they start to form soft peaks, add half the sugar and continue beating until the mixture holds stiff peaks.

3 With a large metal spoon, fold in the remaining sugar and the vanilla or almond extract, if using.

4 Pipe or spoon the mixture on to the prepared baking sheets. Bake them for 2 hours, then turn off the oven. Loosen the meringues, invert, and set in another place on the baking sheets to prevent them from sticking.

5 Leave the meringues in the oven until they are cool. Whip the cream and use to sandwich the meringues together in pairs.

> **Variation**
> To make decorative Meringue Squiggles, line a baking sheet with parchment paper. Make half the amount of meringue mixture given above. Using a large plain nozzle, pipe squiggles about 13cm/5in long on to the baking sheet. Bake for 1 hour. Remove from the oven and leave to cool. Mix the icing sugar with a little water and brush over the meringues. Decorate with sugar sprinkles and serve on their own or with fruit salad and vanilla ice cream.

Energy 78kcal/334kJ; Fat 0.4g, Saturated fat 0g; Carbohydrate 18.9g, Fibre 0.3g

Toasted Oat Meringues

Try these oaty meringues for a lovely crunchy change.

Makes 12
50g/2oz/generous ½ cup rolled oats

2 egg whites
1.5ml/¼ tsp salt
7.5ml/1½ tsp cornflour (cornstarch)
175g/6oz/¾ cup caster (superfine) sugar

1 Preheat the oven to 140°C/275°F/Gas 1. Spread the oats on a baking sheet and toast in the oven until golden. Lower the heat to 120°C/250°F/Gas ½. Grease and flour a baking sheet.

2 Beat the egg whites and salt until they start to form soft peaks. Sift over the cornflour and continue beating until the whites hold stiff peaks. Add half the sugar; whisk until glossy. Add the remaining sugar and fold in carefully. Fold in the toasted oats.

3 Place tablespoonfuls of the mixture on to the baking sheet and bake for 2 hours, then turn off the oven. Turn over the meringues, and leave in the oven until completely cool.

Chewy Walnut Cookies

Makes 18
4 egg whites
275g/10oz/2½ cups icing (confectioners') sugar

5ml/1 tsp cooled strong coffee
115g/4oz/1 cup finely chopped walnuts

1 Preheat the oven to 180°C/350°F/Gas 4. Line two baking sheets with baking parchment and then grease the paper. Using an electric mixer beat the egg whites until frothy. Sift over the icing sugar and add the coffee.

2 Add 15ml/1 tbsp water; beat on low speed to blend, then on high until thick. Fold in the walnuts. Place spoonfuls of the mixture 2.5cm/1in apart on the sheets. Bake for 12–15 minutes. Transfer to a wire rack to cool.

Top: Energy 87kcal/364kJ; Fat 4.2g, Saturated fat 2.6g; Carbohydrate 12.3g; Fibre 0g
Above: Energy 107Kcal/449kJ; Fat 4.4g; Saturated fat 0.4g; Carbohydrate 16.2g; Fibre 0.2g

Chocolate Macaroons

Serve these delicious macaroons with tea.

Makes 24
50g/2oz plain (semisweet) chocolate, melted
175g/6oz/1 cup blanched almonds

225g/8oz/generous 1 cup caster (superfine) sugar
3 egg whites
2.5ml/1/2 tsp vanilla extract
1.5ml/1/4 tsp almond extract
icing (confectioners') sugar, for dusting

1 Preheat the oven to 160°C/325°F/Gas 3. Line two baking sheets with baking parchment and then grease them.

2 Grind the almonds in a food processor. Transfer to a bowl, then blend in the sugar, egg whites, vanilla and almond extracts.

3 Stir in the melted chocolate. The mixture should just hold its shape; if it is too soft, chill for 15 minutes.

4 Shape the mixture into walnut-size balls. Place on the baking sheets and flatten slightly. Brush with a little water and dust with icing sugar. Bake until just firm, 10–12 minutes. With a metal spatula, transfer to a wire rack to cool.

Big Macaroons

Makes 9
2 egg whites
5ml/1 tsp almond extract

115/4oz/1 cup ground almonds
130g/4½oz/1 cup light muscovado (brown) sugar

1 Preheat the oven to 180°C/350°F/Gas 4. Line a large baking sheet with baking parchment. Whisk the egg whites until they form stiff peaks. Add the almond extract and whisk to combine. Fold the almonds and sugar into the mixture.

2 Place nine spoonfuls of the mixture on the baking sheet and flatten slightly. Bake for 15 minutes. Leave to cool on the sheet for 5 minutes before removing to a wire rack to cool completely.

Top: Energy 94kcal/393kJ; Fat 4.7g, Saturated fat 0.7g; Carbohydrate 11.6g; Fibre 0.6g
Above: Energy 138Kcal/577kJ; Fat 7.1g; Saturated fat 0.6g; Carbohydrate 16g; Fibre 0.9g

Coconut Macaroons

Makes 24
40g/1½oz/⅓ cup plain (all-purpose) flour
1.5ml/1¼tsp salt

225g/8oz/4 cups desiccated (dry unsweetened shredded) coconut
170ml/5½fl oz/scant ¾ cup sweetened condensed milk

1 Preheat the oven to 180°C/350°F/Gas 4. Grease two baking sheets. Sift the flour and salt into a bowl and then stir in the coconut. Pour in the condensed milk and mix, stirring from the centre, to form a thick mixture.

2 Drop tablespoonfuls of the mixture 2.5cm/1in apart on the baking sheets. Bake until golden brown, about 20 minutes.

Chocolate Orange Sponge Drops

Light and crispy, with a zesty marmalade filling, these sponge drops are truly delightful.

Makes 14–15
2 eggs
50g/2oz/¼ cup caster (superfine) sugar

2.5ml/½ tsp grated orange rind
50g/2oz/½ cup plain (all-purpose) flour
60ml/4 tbsp fine-shred orange marmalade
40g/1½oz plain (semisweet) chocolate, melted

1 Preheat the oven to 200°C/400°F/Gas 6. Line three baking sheets with baking parchment.

2 Put the eggs and sugar in a bowl over a pan of simmering water. Whisk until thick and pale. Remove from the pan and whisk until cool. Whisk in the orange rind. Sift the flour over and fold it in gently.

3 Put 28–30 dessertspoonfuls of the mixture on the baking sheets. Bake for 8 minutes, until golden. Cool slightly, then transfer to a wire rack. Sandwich pairs together with marmalade. Melt the chocolate and drizzle over the drops.

Top: Energy 86Kcal/357kJ; Fat 6.6g; Saturated fat 5.5g; Carbohydrate 5.8g; Fibre 1.3g
Above: Energy 58kcal/247kJ; Fat 1.5g; Saturated fat 0.7g; Carbohydrate 10.5g; Fibre 0.2g

Crunchy Oat Cookies

Home-made biscuits like these crunchy cookies are always a favourite, and the variations are endless.

Makes 14
175g/6oz/¾ cup butter or margarine, at room temperature
175g/6oz/generous ¾ cup caster (superfine) sugar
1 egg yolk
175g/6oz/1½ cups plain (all-purpose) flour
5ml/1 tsp bicarbonate of soda (baking soda)
2.5ml/½ tsp salt
50g/2oz/⅔ cup rolled oats
50g/2oz/⅔ cup small crunchy nugget cereal

1 Cream the butter or margarine and sugar together until light and fluffy. Mix in the egg yolk.

2 Sift over the flour, bicarbonate of soda and salt, then stir into the butter mixture. Add the oats and cereal, and stir to blend. Chill for at least 20 minutes.

3 Preheat the oven to 190°C/375°F/Gas 5. Grease a large baking sheet.

4 Roll the mixture into balls. Place them on the baking sheet and flatten with the base of a floured glass.

5 Bake until golden, about 10–12 minutes. Then, with a metal spatula, transfer to a wire rack to cool. Store the cookies in an airtight container.

> **Variations**
> • Add grated orange rind to the mixture to give a delicate citrus taste.
> • You can substitute 50g/2oz/¼ cup chopped walnuts or pecan nuts for the cereal to make nutty oatmeal cookies, or try chocolate chips, raisins or sultanas instead.
> • Other dried fruits, such as papaya, also transform the cookies and can be substituted for all or part of the cereal.

Farmhouse Cookies

Delightfully wholesome, these melt-in-the-mouth farmhouse cookies always go down well.

Makes 18
115g/4oz/½ cup butter or margarine, at room temperature
90g/3½oz/7 tbsp soft light brown sugar
65g/2½oz/5 tbsp crunchy peanut butter
1 egg
50g/2oz/½ cup plain (all-purpose) flour
2.5ml/½ tsp baking powder
2.5ml/½ tsp ground cinnamon
1.5ml/¼ tsp salt
175g/6oz/1½ cups muesli (granola)
50g/2oz/½ cup raisins
50g/2oz/½ cup chopped walnuts

1 Preheat the oven to 180°C/350°F/Gas 4. Grease a large baking sheet.

2 Cream the butter or margarine and sugar until light and fluffy. Beat in the peanut butter and then beat in the egg.

3 Sift the flour, baking powder, cinnamon and salt over the peanut butter mixture and stir to blend. Stir in the muesli, raisins and walnuts. Taste the mixture to see if it needs more sugar, as the sugar content of muesli varies.

4 Drop rounded tablespoonfuls of the mixture on to the prepared baking sheet about 2.5cm/1in apart. Press gently with the back of a spoon to spread each mound into a circle.

5 Bake until lightly coloured, about 15 minutes. With a metal spatula, transfer to a wire rack to cool. Store the cookies in an airtight container.

> **Cook's Tip**
> Make these cookies extra wholesome by using a good-quality, rich-tasting peanut butter from your health-food store. You can also use luxury muesli with exotic fruits to make them even tastier.

Energy 165kcal/688kJ; Fat 10g, Saturated fat 4.1g; Carbohydrate 16.9g; Fibre 1.1g

Energy 220kcal/923kJ; Fat 11.9g, Saturated fat 6.8g; Carbohydrate 27.6g; Fibre 0.8g

Nutty Nougat

Makes about 500g/1¼lb

225g/8oz/generous 1 cup
  granulated sugar
225g/8oz/²⁄₃ cup cup clear honey

1 large (US extra large) egg white
115g/4oz/1 cup flaked (sliced)
  almonds or chopped pistachio
  nuts, roasted

1 Line an 18cm/7in square cake tin (pan) with rice paper. Gently heat the sugar and honey with 60ml/4 tbsp water in a heavy pan, stirring until the sugar has completely dissolved.

2 Boil the syrup, without stirring, until soft crack stage (151°C/304°F on a sugar thermometer). Remove from the heat and cool slightly. Whisk the egg white until stiff, then drizzle over the syrup while still whisking. Stir in the nuts. Pour into the tin and leave to cool completely. Cut into squares before it hardens.

Oaty Coconut Cookies

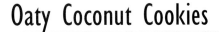

The coconut gives these cookies a wonderful texture.

Makes 48
175g/6oz/generous 2 cups quick-
  cooking oats
75g/3oz/1 cup desiccated (dry
  unsweetened shredded) coconut
225g/8oz/1 cup butter
115g/4oz/generous ½ cup caster
  (superfine) sugar

50g/2oz/¼ cup soft dark
  brown sugar
2 eggs
60ml/4 tbsp milk
7.5ml/1½ tsp vanilla extract
115g/4oz/1 cup plain
  (all-purpose) flour, sifted
2.5ml/½ tsp bicarbonate of soda
  (baking soda)
2.5ml/½ tsp salt
5ml/1 tsp ground cinnamon

1 Preheat the oven to 200°C/400°F/Gas 6. Spread the oats and coconut on a baking sheet. Bake for 8–10 minutes.

2 Cream the butter and sugars. Beat in the eggs, milk and vanilla. Fold in the dry ingredients, and the oats and coconut. Drop spoonfuls of mixture on to two greased baking sheets, and bake for 8–10 minutes. Cool on a wire rack.

Crunchy Jumbles

For even crunchier cookies, add 50g/2oz/½ cup walnuts, coarsely chopped, with the cereal and chocolate chips.

Makes 36
115g/4oz/½ cup butter or
  margarine, at room temperature
225g/8oz/generous 1 cup caster
  (superfine) sugar

1 egg
5ml/1 tsp vanilla extract
150g/5oz/1¼ cups plain
  (all-purpose) flour, sifted
2.5ml/½ tsp bicarbonate of soda
  (baking soda)
1.5ml/¼ tsp salt
50g/2oz/2¼ cups crisped
  rice cereal
175g/6oz/1 cup chocolate chips

1 Preheat the oven to 180°C/350°F/Gas 4. Grease two baking sheets. Cream the butter or margarine and sugar until fluffy. Add the egg and vanilla extract. Add the flour, bicarbonate of soda and the salt, and fold in.

2 Add the cereal and chocolate chips and mix thoroughly. Drop spoonfuls 5cm/2in apart on to baking sheets and bake for 10–12 minutes. Transfer to a wire rack to cool.

Cinnamon Balls

Makes 126
175g/6oz/1½ ground almonds
75g/3oz/scant ½ cup caster
  (superfine) sugar

15ml/1 tbsp ground cinnamon
2 egg whites
icing (confectioners') sugar,
  for dredging

1 Preheat the oven to 180°C/350°F/Gas 4. Grease a large baking sheet. Mix the almonds, sugar and cinnamon in a bowl. Whisk the egg whites until stiff and fold into the almond mixture.

2 Roll small spoonfuls of the mixture into balls and place on the baking sheet. Bake for 15 minutes, then cool on a wire rack. Roll the cooled balls in some sifted icing sugar until completely covered.

Top: Energy 2250Kcal/9511kJ; Fat 64.2g; Saturated fat 5.1g; Carbohydrate 415g; Fibre 8.5g
Above: Energy 84kcal/352kJ; Fat 5.4g, Saturated Fat 3.4g; Carbohydrate 8.3g, Fibre 0.5g

Top: 95kcal/398kJ; Fat 4.2g, Saturated Fat 2.5g; Carbohydrate 14.2g, Fibre 0.3g
Above: Energy 15Kcal/63kJ; Fat 0.8g; Saturated fat 0.1g; Carbohydrate 1.8g; Fibre 0.1g

Ginger Cookies

So much tastier than store-bought varieties, these ginger cookies will disappear quickly, so be sure to make a large batch!

Makes 60
275g/10oz/2½ cups plain (all-purpose) flour
5ml/1 tsp bicarbonate of soda (baking soda)

7.5ml/1½ tsp ground ginger
1.5ml/¼ tsp ground cinnamon
1.5ml/¼ tsp ground cloves
115g/4oz/½ cup butter or margarine, at room temperature
350g/12oz/1¾ cups caster (superfine) sugar
1 egg, beaten
60ml/4 tbsp treacle (molasses)
5ml/1 tsp fresh lemon juice

1 Preheat the oven to 160°C/325°F/Gas 3. Lightly grease three to four baking sheets.

2 Sift the flour, bicarbonate of soda and spices into a small bowl. Set aside.

3 Cream the butter or margarine and two-thirds of the sugar together. Stir in the egg, treacle and lemon juice. Add the flour mixture and mix in thoroughly with a wooden spoon to make a soft dough.

4 Shape the dough into 2cm/¾in balls. Roll the balls in the remaining sugar and place about 5cm/2in apart on the prepared baking sheets.

5 Bake until the cookies are just firm to the touch, about 12 minutes. With a metal spatula, transfer the cookies to a wire rack and leave to cool. The biscuits will firm up as they cool.

Variation
Coarsely chop 150g/5oz drained preserved stem ginger. Add 115g/4oz to the cookie mixture at the end of step 3, and press the remaining pieces into the top of each of the cookies at the end of step 4.

Cream Cheese Spirals

These spirals look so impressive and melt in the mouth, yet they are surprisingly easy to make.

Makes 32
225g/8oz/1 cup butter, at room temperature
225g/8oz/1 cup cream cheese
10ml/2 tsp caster (superfine) sugar
225g/8oz/2 cups plain (all-purpose) flour

1 egg white, beaten with 15ml/1 tbsp water, for glazing
caster sugar, for sprinkling

For the filling
115g/4oz/1 cup finely chopped walnuts
115g/4oz/¾ cup soft light brown sugar
5ml/1 tsp ground cinnamon

1 Cream the butter, cream cheese and sugar until soft. Sift over the flour and mix until combined. Gather into a ball and divide in half. Flatten each half, wrap in baking parchment and chill for 30 minutes.

2 Meanwhile, make the filling. Mix the chopped walnuts with the light brown sugar and cinnamon, stirring well so that the nuts are well coated with the spices. Set aside.

3 Preheat the oven to 190°C/375°F/Gas 5. Grease two baking sheets. Working with one half of the dough at a time, roll out thinly into a 28cm/11in circle. Using a dinner plate as a guide, trim the edges with a knife.

4 Brush the surface with the egg-white glaze, and then sprinkle evenly with half the filling.

5 Cut the circle into 16 triangular segments. Starting from the base of a triangle, roll up the dough to form a spiral. Repeat with the remaining triangles.

6 Place the spirals on the prepared baking sheets and brush with the remaining egg and water glaze. Sprinkle with caster sugar. Bake until golden, about 15–20 minutes. Cool on a wire rack.

Energy 57kcal/239kJ; Fat 1.7g, Saturated fat 1g; Carbohydrate 10.3g; Fibre 0.1g

Energy 150kcal/621kJ; Fat 11.8g, Saturated fat 6g; Carbohydrate 9.7g; Fibre 0.3g

Raspberry Sandwich Cookies

These cookies may be stored in an airtight container with sheets of baking parchment between the layers.

Makes 32
175g/6oz/1 cup blanched almonds
175g/6oz/1½ cups plain
　(all-purpose) flour
175g/6oz/¾ cup butter,
　at room temperature
115g/4oz/generous ½ cup caster
　(superfine) sugar
grated rind of 1 lemon
5ml/1 tsp vanilla extract
1 egg white
1.5ml/¼ tsp salt
25g/1oz/¼ cup flaked
　(sliced) almonds
250ml/8fl oz/1 cup
　raspberry jam
15ml/1 tbsp lemon juice

1 Process the blanched almonds and 45ml/3 tbsp flour in a food processor or blender until finely ground. Cream the butter and sugar together until light and fluffy. Stir in the lemon rind and vanilla. Add the ground almonds and remaining flour, and mix well. Gather into a ball, wrap in baking parchment, and chill for 1 hour.

2 Preheat the oven to 160°C/325°F/Gas 3. Line two baking sheets with baking parchment. Divide the cookie mixture into four equal parts. Working with one section at a time, roll out to a thickness of 3mm/⅛in on a lightly floured surface.

3 With a 6cm/2½in fluted pastry (cookie) cutter, stamp out circles. Using a 2cm/¾in piping (icing) nozzle or pastry cutter, stamp out the centres from half the circles. Place the rings and circles 2.5cm/1in apart on the baking sheets.

4 Whisk the egg white with the salt until just frothy. Chop the flaked almonds. Brush the cookie rings with the egg white, then sprinkle over the almonds. Bake until lightly browned, about 12–15 minutes. Cool for a few minutes on the baking sheets then transfer to a wire rack.

5 In a pan, melt the jam with the lemon juice until it comes to a simmer. Brush the jam over the cookie circles and sandwich together with the rings.

Energy 133kcal/554kJ; Fat 8.1g, Saturated fat 3.1g; Carbohydrate 13.9g; Fibre 0.6g

Christmas Cookies

Decorate these delicious cookies with festive decorations or make them at any time of year.

Makes 30
175g/6oz/¾ cup unsalted
　(sweet) butter, at room
　temperature
275g/10oz/1½ cups caster
　(superfine) sugar
1 egg
1 egg yolk
5ml/1 tsp vanilla extract
grated rind of 1 lemon
1.5ml/¼ tsp salt
275g/10oz/2½ cups plain
　(all-purpose) flour

For decorating (optional)
175g/6oz/1½ cups icing
　(confectioners') sugar
food colouring
small decorations

1 Preheat the oven to 180°C/350°F/Gas 4. With an electric mixer, cream the butter until soft. Add the sugar gradually and continue beating until light and fluffy.

2 Using a wooden spoon, slowly mix in the whole egg and the egg yolk. Add the vanilla extract, lemon rind and salt. Stir to mix well. Add the flour and stir until blended.

3 Gather the mixture into a ball, wrap in baking parchment and chill for 30 minutes.

4 On a floured surface, roll out the mixture about 3mm/⅛in thick. Stamp out shapes or rounds with cookie cutters. Bake until lightly coloured, about 8 minutes. Transfer to a wire rack and leave to cool completely. The cookies can be left plain, or iced and decorated.

5 To ice the cookies, mix the icing sugar with enough water to make a thick icing consistency. Add a few drops of food colouring to create just one colour, or divide the mixture into small amounts and add different food colouring to each.

6 Fill a piping (icing) bag fitted with a fine nozzle with the icing and pipe dots, lines and patterns on to the cookies. Finish with small decorations such as edible silver balls.

Energy 118kcal/495kJ; Fat 5.3g, Saturated fat 3.2g; Carbohydrate 17.3g; Fibre 0.3g

Chocolate Pretzels

Pretzels come in many different flavours – here is a delicious chocolate version that is guaranteed to please the tastebuds.

Makes 28

150g/5oz/1¼ cups plain (all-purpose) flour
1.5ml/¼ tsp salt
20g/¾oz/3 tbsp unsweetened cocoa powder
115g/4oz/½ cup butter, at room temperature
130g/4½oz/scant ¾ cup caster (superfine) sugar
1 egg
1 egg white, lightly beaten, for glazing
sugar crystals, for sprinkling

1 Sift together the flour, salt and cocoa powder. Set aside. Cream the butter until light. Add the sugar and continue beating until light and fluffy. Beat in the egg.

2 Add the dry ingredients and stir to blend thoroughly. Gather the dough into a ball, wrap it in clear film (plastic wrap) and chill for 1 hour.

3 Roll the dough into 28 small balls. Chill the balls until needed. Preheat the oven to 190°C/375°F/Gas 5. Lightly grease two baking sheets.

4 Roll each ball into a rope about 25cm/10in long. With each rope, form a loop with the two ends facing you. Twist the ends and fold them back on to the circle, pressing them in to make a pretzel shape. Place on the prepared baking sheets.

5 Brush each of the pretzels with the egg white. Sprinkle sugar crystals over the tops and bake in the oven until firm, about 10–12 minutes. Using a metal spatula, transfer to a wire rack to cool.

Variation
To make mocha-flavoured pretzels, replace 10ml/1 tsp of the unsweetened cocoa powder with instant coffee powder.

Iced Ginger Cookies

If your children enjoy cooking with you, mixing and rolling the dough, or cutting out different shapes, this is the ideal recipe to let them practise on.

Makes 16

115g/4oz/½ cup soft light brown sugar
115g/4oz/½ cup soft margarine
a pinch of salt
a few drops of vanilla extract
175g/6oz/1½ cups wholemeal flour
15g/½oz/2 tbsp unsweetened cocoa powder, sifted
10ml/2 tsp ground ginger
a little milk
glacé icing and glacé (candied) cherries, to decorate

1 Preheat the oven to 190°C/375°F/Gas 5. Grease two baking sheets. Cream the light brown sugar, margarine, salt and vanilla extract together until very soft and light.

2 Work in the flour, cocoa and ginger, adding a little milk, if necessary, to bind the mixture. Knead lightly on a floured surface until smooth.

3 Roll out the dough on a lightly floured surface to about 5mm/¼in thick. Stamp out shapes using cookie cutters and place on baking sheets.

4 Bake the cookies for 10–15 minutes, leave to cool on the baking sheets until firm, then transfer to a wire rack to cool completely. Decorate the cooled cookies with the glacé icing and glacé cherries.

Cook's Tip
This mixture is ideal for creating small gingerbread people, which children will love to make. Cut out the cookies using appropriate cutters and decorate with raisins for eyes and glacé (candied) cherries for a smiley mouth. Sesame seeds can be pressed into the mixture to make a pattern or the outline of clothing. Or pipe icing on to the finished cookies to make features, buttons, a bow tie or scarf and clothes.

Energy 72kcal/303kJ; Fat 3.8g, Saturated fat 2.3g; Carbohydrate 9.1g; Fibre 0.3g

Energy 119kcal/497kJ; Fat 6.4g, Saturated fat 3.9g; Carbohydrate 14.7g; Fibre 1.1g

Peanut Butter Cookies

These moreish cookies must come close to the top of the list of America's favourites. They are quick and simple to make with ingredients that you will normally have in the store cupboard or pantry.

Makes 24

150g/5oz/1¼ cups plain (all-purpose) flour
2.5ml/½ tsp bicarbonate of soda (baking soda)
2.5ml/½ tsp salt
115g/4oz/½ cup butter, at room temperature
170g/5¾oz/generous ⅔ cup soft light brown sugar
1 egg
5ml/1 tsp vanilla extract
260g/9½oz/scant 1¼ cups crunchy peanut butter

1 Sift together the flour, bicarbonate of soda and salt, and set aside. In another bowl, cream the butter and sugar together until light and fluffy.

2 In a third bowl, mix the egg and vanilla, then gradually beat into the butter mixture. Stir in the peanut butter and blend thoroughly. Stir in the dry ingredients. Chill for 30 minutes, or until firm.

3 Preheat the oven to 180°C/350°F/Gas 4. Grease two baking sheets. Spoon out rounded teaspoonfuls of the dough and roll into balls.

4 Place the balls on the baking sheets and press flat with a fork into circles about 6cm/2½in in diameter, making a criss-cross pattern.

5 Bake in the oven until lightly coloured, about 12–15 minutes. Using a metal spatula transfer to a wire rack to cool.

Variation
For extra crunch add 50g/2oz/½ cup chopped raw, skinned peanuts with the peanut butter at step 2. (Raw peanuts do not keep well so always buy in small quantities.)

Chocolate Chip Cookies

A perennial favourite with all the family, these cookies contain walnuts as well as chocolate chips.

Makes 24

115g/4oz/½ cup butter or margarine, at room temperature
45g/1¾ oz/scant ¼ cup caster (superfine) sugar
100g/3¾oz/scant ½ cup soft dark brown sugar
1 egg
2.5ml/½ tsp vanilla extract
175g/6oz/1½ cups plain (all-purpose) flour
2.5ml/½ tsp bicarbonate of soda (baking soda)
1.5ml/¼ tsp salt
175g/6oz/1 cup chocolate chips
50g/2oz/⅓ cup walnuts, chopped

1 Preheat the oven to 180°C/350°F/Gas 4. Lightly grease two large baking sheets. With an electric mixer, cream the butter or margarine and both the sugars together until light and fluffy.

2 In another bowl, mix the egg and the vanilla extract, then gradually beat into the butter mixture. Sift over the flour, bicarbonate of soda and salt and stir. Add the chocolate chips and walnuts, and mix to combine well.

3 Place heaped teaspoonfuls of the dough 5cm/2in apart on the baking sheets. Bake in the oven until lightly coloured, about 10–15 minutes. Transfer to a wire rack to cool.

Variations
All chocolate: substitute 15ml/1tbsp unsweetened cocoa powder for the same quantity of flour, and omit the vanilla.
Mocha: Use coffee essence instead of vanilla extract.
Macadamia nut or hazelnut: instead of the walnuts add whole or coarsely chopped macadamia nuts or hazelnuts.
Dried fruit: instead of the walnuts and chocolate chips add chopped dried fruit, such as rains, sultanas (golden raisins), glacé (candied) cherries, or tropical fruit.
Banana: substitute a ripe, mashed banana and 50g/2oz/¼ cup chopped banana chips for the walnuts and chocolate chips.

Energy 154kcal/641kJ; Fat 9.9g, Saturated fat 4g; Carbohydrate 13.7g; Fibre 0.8g

Energy 139kcal/582kJ; Fat 7.7g, Saturated fat 3.9g; Carbohydrate 16.7g; Fibre 0.5g

Brittany Butter Cookies

These little cookies are similar to shortbread, but they are richer in taste and texture.

Makes 18–20
6 egg yolks, lightly beaten
15ml/1 tbsp milk

250g/9oz/2¼ cups plain
    (all-purpose) flour
175g/6oz/generous ¾ cup caster
    (superfine) sugar
200g/7oz/scant 1 cup lightly
    salted butter at room
    temperature, cut into
    small pieces

1 Preheat the oven to 180°C/350°F/Gas 4. Lightly butter a large baking sheet. Mix 15ml/1 tbsp of the egg yolks with the milk for a glaze. Set aside.

2 Sift the flour into a large bowl and make a central well. Add the egg yolks, sugar and butter and, using your fingertips, work them together until smooth and creamy. Gradually blend in the flour to form a smooth but slightly sticky dough.

3 Using floured hands, pat out the dough to 8mm/⅓in thick and cut out circles using a 7.5cm/3in cookie cutter.

4 Transfer the circles to the baking sheet, brush with egg glaze, then score to create a lattice pattern.

5 Bake for 12–15 minutes, or until golden. Cool on the baking sheet on a wire rack for 15 minutes, then transfer to the wire rack to cool completely.

> **Variation**
> To make a large Brittany Butter Cake, pat the dough with well-floured hands into a greased 23cm/9in loose-based cake tin (pan) or springform tin. Brush with the egg and milk glaze, and score the lattice pattern on the top. Bake for 45–60 minutes, or until firm to the touch and golden brown. Cool in the tin for 15 minutes before carefully turning out on to a rack to cool completely.

Festive Cookies

Dainty, hand-painted cookies look delightful served at Christmas. These are great fun for children to make as presents, and any shape of cookie cutter can be used.

Makes about 12
75g/3oz/6 tbsp butter
50g/2oz/½ cup icing
    (confectioners') sugar

finely grated rind of 1
    small lemon
1 egg yolk
175g/6oz/1½ cups plain
    (all-purpose) flour
a pinch of salt

To decorate
2 egg yolks
red and green
    food colouring

1 Beat the butter, icing sugar and lemon rind together until pale and fluffy. Beat in the egg yolk, and then sift in the flour and the salt. Knead together to form a smooth dough. Wrap and chill for 30 minutes.

2 Preheat the oven to 190°C/375°F/Gas 5 and lightly grease two baking sheets.

3 On a lightly floured surface, roll out the dough to 3mm/⅛in thick. Using a 6cm/2½in fluted cutter, stamp out as many cookies as you can, with the cutter dipped in flour to prevent it from sticking to the dough.

4 Transfer the cookies to the prepared baking sheets. Mark the tops lightly with a 2.5cm/1in holly leaf cutter and use a 5mm/¼in plain piping (icing) nozzle for the berries. Chill for 10 minutes, until firm.

5 Meanwhile, to make the decoration put each egg yolk into a small cup. Mix red food colouring into one and green food colouring into the other. Using a small, clean paintbrush, carefully paint the colours on to the cookies.

6 Bake for 10–12 minutes, or until they begin to colour around the edges. Let them cool slightly on the baking sheets, then transfer to a wire rack to cool completely.

Energy 59kcal/246kJ; Fat 4.1g, Saturated fat 1.1g; Carbohydrate 4.5g; Fibre 0.4g

Energy 118kcal/494kJ; Fat 5.8g, Saturated fat 3.4g; Carbohydrate 15.7g; Fibre 0.5g

Traditional Sugar Cookies

These lovely old-fashioned cookies make a tasty snack.

Makes 36
350g/12oz/3 cups plain
   (all-purpose) flour
5ml/1 tsp bicarbonate of soda
   (baking soda)
10ml/2 tsp baking powder
1.5ml/¼ tsp freshly
   grated nutmeg
115g/4oz/½ cup butter or
   margarine, at room temperature
225g/8oz/generous 1 cup caster
   (superfine) sugar
2.5ml/½ tsp vanilla extract
1 egg
120ml/4fl oz/½ cup milk
coloured or demerara (raw) sugar,
   for sprinkling

1 Sift the flour, bicarbonate of soda, baking powder and nutmeg into a small bowl. Set aside. Cream the butter or margarine, caster sugar and vanilla extract together until the mixture is light and fluffy. Add the egg and beat to mix well.

2 Add the flour mixture alternately with the milk, stirring with a wooden spoon to make a soft dough. Wrap the dough in clear film and chill for 30 minutes.

3 Preheat the oven to 180°C/350°F/Gas 4. Roll out the dough on a lightly floured surface to a 3mm/⅛in thickness. Cut into circles with a cookie cutter.

4 Transfer the cookies to ungreased baking sheets. Sprinkle each one with sugar. Bake until golden, 10–12 minutes. With a metal spatula, transfer the cookies to a wire rack to cool.

> **Variation**
> *Transform these cookies into funky flower-power cookies for a children's party by omitting the final sprinkling of sugar and icing them when cold. Spoon a little icing on to the top of each cookie and spread into a circle, then top with a sugared flower. Choose wildly contrasting colours or dainty pastel shades for the icings and flowers.*

Energy 85kcal/359kJ; Fat 3g, Saturated fat 1.8g; Carbohydrate 14.3g; Fibre 0.3g

Spiced Cookies

Try these warmly spiced cookies and you are sure to be pleasantly surprised by their fabulous flavour. They are also very quick and easy to make.

Makes 48
200g/7oz/1¾ cups plain
   (all-purpose) flour
50g/2oz/½ cup cornflour
   (cornstarch)
10ml/2 tsp baking powder
2.5ml/½ tsp ground cardamom
2.5ml/½ tsp ground cinnamon
2.5ml/½ tsp freshly
   grated nutmeg
2.5ml/½ tsp ground ginger
2.5ml/½ tsp ground allspice
2.5ml/½ tsp salt
2.5ml/½ tsp freshly ground
   black pepper
225g/8oz/1 cup butter
   or margarine, at
   room temperature
90g/3½oz/scant ½ cup soft
   light brown sugar
2.5ml/½ tsp vanilla extract
5ml/1 tsp finely grated
   lemon rind
50ml/2fl oz/¼ cup whipping
   cream
75g/3oz/¾ cup finely
   ground almonds
50ml/2 tbsp icing
   (confectioners') sugar

1 Preheat the oven to 180°C/350°F/Gas 4. Sift the flour, cornflour, baking powder, spices, salt and pepper into a bowl. Set aside.

2 Using an electric mixer, cream the butter or margarine and brown sugar until light and fluffy. Beat in the vanilla extract and lemon rind.

3 With the mixer on low speed, add the flour mixture alternately with the cream, beginning and ending with flour. Stir in the ground almonds.

4 Shape the dough into 2cm/¾in balls. Place them on ungreased baking sheets about 2.5cm/1in apart. Bake until golden brown underneath, about 15–20 minutes.

5 Leave to cool on the baking sheets for about 1 minute before transferring to a wire rack to cool completely. Before serving, sprinkle lightly with icing sugar.

Energy 75kcal/314kJ; Fat 5.2g, Saturated fat 2.8g; Carbohydrate 6.8g; Fibre 0.2g

Easter Cookies

Traditionally butter could not be eaten during the Lenten fast, so these cookies were a welcome Easter treat.

Makes 16–18

115g/4oz/½ cup butter
or margarine
75g/3oz/scant ½ cup caster
(superfine) sugar, plus extra
for sprinkling

1 egg, separated
200g/7oz/1¾ cups plain
(all-purpose) flour
2.5ml/½ tsp mixed (apple
pie) spice
2.5ml/½ tsp ground cinnamon
50g/2oz/¼ cup currants
15ml/1 tbsp mixed chopped
(candied) peel
15–30ml/1–2 tbsp milk

1 Preheat the oven to 200°C/400°F/Gas 6. Lightly grease two baking sheets. Cream together the butter or margarine and sugar until light and fluffy, then beat in the egg yolk.

2 Sift the flour, mixed spice and cinnamon over the egg mixture in the bowl, then fold in with the currants and chopped mixed peel, adding sufficient milk to make a fairly soft dough.

3 Turn the dough on to a floured surface, knead lightly until just smooth, then roll out using a floured rolling pin, to about a 5mm/¼in thickness. Cut the dough into circles using a 5cm/2in fluted cookie cutter. Transfer the circles to the baking sheets and bake for 10 minutes.

4 Beat the egg white, then brush over the cookies. Sprinkle with caster sugar and return to the oven for a further 10 minutes, until golden. Using a metal spatula transfer to a wire rack to cool.

> **Cook's Tip**
> *Cinnamon is one of the exceptions to the rule that you should, if possible, buy spices whole and grind them freshly when you need them. Although cinnamon sticks are widely available, they are difficult – almost impossible – to grind yourself.*

Melting Moments

These cookies are very crisp and light – and they really do melt in your mouth.

Makes 16–20

40g/1½oz/3 tbsp butter
or margarine
65g/2½oz/5 tbsp lard or
white cooking fat

75g/3oz/scant ½ cup caster
(superfine) sugar
½ egg, beaten
a few drops of vanilla or
almond extract
150g/5oz/1¼ cups self-raising
(self-rising) flour
rolled oats, for coating
4–5 glacé (candied) cherries,
quartered, to decorate

1 Preheat the oven to 180°C/350°F/Gas 4, and grease two baking sheets.

2 Beat together the butter or margarine, lard and sugar, then gradually beat in the egg and vanilla or almond extract.

3 Stir the flour into the beaten mixture, with floured hands, then roll into 16–20 small balls. Spread the rolled oats on a sheet of baking parchment and toss the balls in them to coat evenly.

4 Place the balls, spaced slightly apart, on the baking sheets, place a piece of cherry on top of each and bake for about 15–20 minutes, or until lightly browned.

5 Allow the cookies to cool on the sheets for 5 minutes before transferring to a wire rack to cool completely.

> **Cook's Tips**
> • *The meltingly short texture for these cookies is achieved by using two different kinds of fat. Lard, made from processed pure pork fat, is often used to make light pastries; use a vegetarian white cooking fat (shortening) if you prefer. The butter adds richness and flavour.*
> • *To halve an egg, beat a whole egg in a measuring jug (cup) and then pour off half.*

Shortbread

Once you have tasted this shortbread, you'll never buy a packet from a shop again.

Makes 8
150g/5oz/generous ½ cup unsalted (sweet) butter, at room temperature

115g/4oz/generous ½ cup caster (superfine) sugar
150g/5oz/1¼ cups plain (all-purpose) flour
65g/2½oz/generous ½ cup rice flour
1.5ml/¼ tsp baking powder
1.5ml/¼ tsp salt

1 Preheat the oven to 160°C/325°F/Gas 3. Lightly grease a 20cm/8in shallow round cake tin (pan) or an 18cm/7in square tin and set aside until needed.

2 Cream the butter and sugar together until light and fluffy. Sift over the flours, baking powder and salt, and mix well.

3 Press the mixture neatly into the prepared tin, smoothing the surface with the back of a spoon. Prick all over with a fork, then score into eight equal wedges or into fingers.

4 Bake until golden, about 40–45 minutes. Leave in the tin until cool enough to handle, then unmould and recut the wedges while still hot. Store in an airtight container.

Variation
To make a party sensation for children – Jewelled Shortbread Fingers – bake the shortbread in a greased 18cm/7in square tin (pan). Score the shortbread into fingers when warm and cut when cold. (Use a serrated knife and a sawing action to cut the shortbread neatly.) Make a fairly thin icing using 150g/5oz/ 1¼ cups icing (confectioners') sugar mixed with 10–15ml/ 2–3 tbsp lemon juice, and use to drizzle over the shortbread fingers in a random zigzag pattern. Crush some brightly coloured boiled sweets (hard candies) using a rolling pin and sprinkle them over the icing so that they stick. Add a few gold or silver edible balls to each decorated finger.

Energy 290kcal/1212kJ; Fat 15.7g, Saturated fat 9.8g; Carbohydrate 36.2g; Fibre 0.8g

Flapjacks

For a spicier version, add 5ml/1 tsp ground ginger to the melted butter.

Makes 8
50g/2oz/¼ cup butter

20ml/1 rounded tbsp golden (light corn) syrup
65g/2½oz/scant ½ cup soft dark brown sugar
115g/4oz/⅔ cup rolled oats
1.5ml/¼ tsp salt

1 Preheat the oven to 180°C/350°F/Gas 4. Line and grease a 20cm/8in shallow round cake tin (pan) or an 18cm/7in square tin. Place the butter, golden syrup and sugar in a pan over a low heat. Cook, stirring, until melted and combined.

2 Remove from the heat and add the oats and salt. Stir the mixture to blend. Spoon the mixture into the prepared tin and smooth the surface. Place in the centre of the oven and bake until golden brown, 20–25 minutes.

3 Leave in the tin until cool enough to handle, then unmould and cut into wedges or fingers while still hot. Store in an airtight container.

Variations
*Let your imagination go wild with variations on the flapjack theme.
Apricot and Pecan: substitute maple syrup for the golden (light corn) syrup and add 50g/2oz/½ cup chopped pecan nuts and 50g/2oz/¼ cup chopped ready-to-eat dried apricots.
Lemon: substitute Demerara (raw) sugar for the soft dark brown sugar and add the juice and grated rind of 1 lemon.
Honey and seed: substitute honey for the golden (light corn) syrup and add 30ml/2 tbsp sesame or sunflower seeds.
Fruit: add 50g/2oz/scant ½ cup raisins, sultanas (golden raisins) or dried tropical fruit.
Chocolate: add 50g/2oz chocolate drops or chopped chocolate with some dried fruit as well, if you like.
Apple: add a peeled and cored apple cut into small pieces for a softer flapjack.*

Energy 144kcal/604kJ; Fat 6.4g, Saturated fat 3.3g; Carbohydrate 21g; Fibre 1g

Chunky Chocolate Drops

Do not allow these cookies to cool completely on the baking sheet or they will break when you lift them.

Makes 18

175g/6oz plain (semisweet) chocolate
115g/4oz/½ cup unsalted (sweet) butter
2 eggs
90g/3½oz/½ cup caster (superfine) sugar
50g/2oz/¼ cup (packed) soft light brown sugar
40g/1½oz/⅓ cup plain (all-purpose) flour
25g/1oz/¼ cup unsweetened cocoa powder
5ml/1 tsp baking powder
10ml/2 tsp vanilla extract
pinch of salt
115g/4oz/⅔ cup pecan nuts, toasted and coarsely chopped
175g/6oz/1 cup plain (semisweet) chocolate chips
115g/4oz fine quality white chocolate, chopped into 5mm/¼in pieces
115g/4oz fine quality milk chocolate, chopped into 5mm/¼in pieces

1 Preheat the oven to 160°C/325°F/Gas 3. Grease two large baking sheets.

2 In a medium pan over a low heat, melt the plain chocolate and butter until smooth, stirring frequently. Remove from the heat to cool slightly.

3 Beat the eggs with the sugars until pale and creamy. Gradually beat in the melted chocolate mixture. Beat in the flour, cocoa, baking powder, vanilla extract and salt, until just blended. Add the nuts, chocolate chips and white chocolate pieces.

4 Drop 4–6 heaped tablespoonfuls of the mixture on to each baking sheet 10cm/4in apart and flatten each to a round about 7.5cm/3in. Bake for 8–10 minutes, or until the tops are shiny and cracked and the edges look crisp.

5 Cool the cookies on the baking sheets for about 2 minutes, or until they are just set, then remove them to a wire rack to cool completely.

Chocolate Crackle-tops

These dainty treats are always popular and are best eaten on the day they are baked, as they dry slightly on storage.

Makes 38

200g/7oz plain (semisweet) chocolate, chopped
90g/3½oz/7 tbsp unsalted (sweet) butter
115g/4oz/generous ½ cup caster (superfine) sugar
3 eggs
5ml/1 tsp vanilla extract
215g/7½oz/scant 2 cups plain (all-purpose) flour
25g/1oz/¼ cup unsweetened cocoa powder
2.5ml/½ tsp baking powder
a pinch of salt
175g/6oz/1½ cups icing (confectioners') sugar, for coating

1 Heat the chocolate and butter over a low heat until smooth, stirring frequently. Remove from the heat. Stir in the sugar, and continue stirring until dissolved. Add the eggs, one at a time, beating well after each addition; stir in the vanilla.

2 In a separate bowl, sift together the flour, cocoa, baking powder and salt. Gradually stir into the chocolate mixture until just blended. Cover and chill for at least 1 hour.

3 Preheat the oven to 160°C/325°F/Gas 3. Grease two or three large baking sheets. Place the icing sugar in a small, deep bowl. Using a teaspoon, scoop the dough into small balls and roll in your hands into 4cm/1½in balls.

4 Drop the balls, one at a time, into the icing sugar and roll until heavily coated. Remove each ball with a slotted spoon and tap against the bowl to remove any excess sugar. Place on the baking sheets 4cm/1½in apart.

5 Bake the cookies for 10–15 minutes, or until the tops feel slightly firm when touched with your fingertip.

6 Remove the baking sheets to a wire rack for 2–3 minutes, then remove the cookies to the wire rack to cool.

Energy 301kcal/1256kJ; Fat 20g, Saturated fat 9.7g; Carbohydrate 28.4g; Fibre 1g

Energy 102kcal/428kJ; Fat 4.1g, Saturated fat 2.3g; Carbohydrate 15.8g; Fibre 0.4g

Chocolate and Coconut Slices

These are easier to slice if
they cool overnight.

Makes 24

175g/6oz/2 cups crushed digestive
  cookies (graham crackers)
50g/2oz/¼ cup caster
  (superfine) sugar
a pinch of salt
115g/4oz/½ cup butter or
  margarine, melted
75g/3oz/1 cup desiccated (dry
  unsweetened shredded) coconut
250g/9oz plain (semisweet)
  chocolate chips
250ml/8fl oz/1 cup sweetened
  condensed milk
115g/4oz/1 cup chopped walnuts

1 Preheat the oven to 180°C/350°F/Gas 4. In a bowl,
combine the crushed digestive cookies, sugar, salt and butter
or margarine. Press the mixture evenly over the base of an
ungreased 33 x 23cm/13 x 9in baking dish.

2 Sprinkle the coconut over the cookie base, then scatter over
the chocolate chips. Pour the condensed milk evenly over the
chocolate. Sprinkle the walnuts on top. Bake in the oven for
30 minutes. Unmould and leave to cool before slicing.

Coconut Pyramids

Makes 15

225g/8oz/1 cup desiccated
  (dry unsweetened
  shredded) coconut
115g/4oz/generous ½ cup caster
  (superfine) sugar
2 egg whites

1 Preheat the oven to 190°C/375°F/Gas 5. Grease a baking
sheet. Mix together the coconut and sugar. Lightly whisk the egg
whites and fold enough into the coconut to make a firm mixture.

2 Form teaspoonfuls of the mixture into pyramids. Flatten the
base and press the top into a point. Place on the baking sheet
and bake for 12–15 minutes on a low shelf; the tips should be
golden. Use a metal spatula to loosen them but let them cool
on the baking sheet before transferring to a wire rack.

Top: Energy 55kcal/233kJ; Fat 2.6g, Saturated fat 1.5g; Carbohydrate 7.8g; Fibre 0.2g
Above: Energy 122Kcal/509kJ; Fat 9.3g; Saturated fat 8g; Carbohydrate 9g; Fibre 2.1g

Chocolate Chip Oat Cookies

Oat cookies are given a
delicious lift by the inclusion
of chocolate chips. Try
caramel chips for a change,
if you like.

Makes 60

115g/4oz/1 cup plain
  (all-purpose) flour
2.5ml/½ tsp bicarbonate of soda
  (baking soda)
1.5ml/¼ tsp baking powder
1.5ml/¼ tsp salt
115g/4oz/½ cup butter or
  margarine, at room temperature
115g/4oz/generous ½ cup caster
  (superfine) sugar
90g/3½oz/scant ½ cup soft light
  brown sugar
1 egg
2.5ml/½ tsp vanilla extract
75g/3oz/scant 1 cup rolled oats
175g/6oz/1 cup plain (semisweet)
  chocolate chips

1 Preheat the oven to 180°C/350°F/Gas 4. Grease three or
four baking sheets. Sift the flour, bicarbonate of soda, baking
powder and salt into a mixing bowl. Set aside.

2 With an electric mixer, cream the butter or margarine and
the sugars together. Add the egg and vanilla, and beat until light
and fluffy.

3 Add the flour mixture to the egg and vanilla, and beat on low
speed until thoroughly blended. Stir in the rolled oats and plain
chocolate chips, mixing well with a wooden spoon. The dough
should be crumbly.

4 Drop heaped teaspoonfuls on to the baking sheets, about
2.5cm/1in apart. Bake until just firm around the edges but still
soft in the centres, about 15 minutes. With a metal spatula,
transfer the cookies to a wire rack to cool.

> **Variation**
> *For an elegant look suitable to accompany a chilled dessert, melt
> plain (semisweet) chocolate over a pan of hot, but not boiling
> water, stirring until smooth. Dip each baked cookie into the chocolate
> to cover one half of the cookie. Leave to set before serving.*

Energy 217kcal/907kJ; Fat 14.6g, Saturated fat 7.5g; Carbohydrate 20g; Fibre 1g

Nutty Chocolate Squares

These delicious squares are incredibly rich, so cut them smaller if you wish.

Makes 16

2 eggs
10ml/2 tsp vanilla extract
1.5ml/¼ tsp salt
175g/6oz/1 cup pecan nuts, coarsely chopped

50g/2oz/½ cup plain (all-purpose) flour
50g/2oz/¼ cup caster (superfine) sugar
120ml/4fl oz/½ cup golden (light corn) syrup
75g/3oz plain (semisweet) chocolate, finely chopped
40g/1½oz/3 tbsp butter
16 pecan nut halves, to decorate

1 Preheat the oven to 160°C/325°F/Gas 3. Line the base and sides of a 20cm/8in square baking tin (pan) with baking parchment and lightly grease the paper.

2 Whisk together the eggs, vanilla extract and salt. In another bowl, mix together the chopped pecan nuts and flour. Set both aside until needed.

3 In a pan, bring the sugar and golden syrup to the boil. Watch it carefully and remove from the heat as soon as it comes to the boil. Stir in the chocolate and butter, and blend thoroughly with a wooden spoon. Mix in the beaten egg mixture, then fold in the pecan nut mixture.

4 Pour the mixture into the baking tin and bake until set, about 35 minutes. Cool in the tin for 10 minutes before unmoulding.

5 Cut into 5cm/2in squares and press pecan nut halves into the tops while warm. Cool on a wire rack.

> **Variation**
> *Toasted hazelnuts also taste great in place of the pecan nuts. Simply brown the hazelnuts under a hot grill (broiler), turning them every so often.. When toasted all over, leave to cool, then rub them in a clean dish towel until the skins are removed.*

Raisin Brownies

Cover these divine fruity brownies with a light chocolate frosting for an extra treat, if you like.

Makes 16

115g/4oz/½ cup butter or margarine
50g/2oz/½ cup unsweetened cocoa powder

2 eggs
225g/8oz/generous 1 cup caster (superfine) sugar
5ml/1 tsp vanilla extract
40g/1½oz/⅓ cup plain (all-purpose) flour
75g/3oz/¾ cup finely chopped walnuts
75g/3oz/generous ½ cup raisins

1 Preheat the oven to 180°C/350°F/Gas 4. Line the base and sides of a 20cm/8in square baking tin (pan) with baking parchment and grease the paper.

2 Gently melt the butter or margarine in a small pan. Remove from the heat and stir in the cocoa powder.

3 With an electric mixer, beat the eggs, caster sugar and vanilla extract together until light. Add the cocoa and butter mixture and stir to blend.

4 Sift the flour over the cocoa mixture and gently fold in. Do not overmix.

5 Add the walnuts and raisins, and scrape the mixture into the prepared baking tin.

6 Bake in the centre of the oven for 30 minutes. Leave in the tin to cool before cutting into 5cm/2in squares and removing from the tin. The brownies should be soft and moist.

> **Cook's Tip**
> *Adding dried fruit makes brownies a little more substantial and adds to their delicious flavour. Try to find Californian or Spanish raisins for the best flavour and texture.*

Energy 172kcal/719kJ; Fat 11.8g, Saturated fat 2.9g; Carbohydrate 15.2g; Fibre 0.7g

Energy 181kcal/759kJ; Fat 10.5g, Saturated fat 4.6g; Carbohydrate 20.4g; Fibre 0.7g

White Chocolate Brownies

If you wish, toasted and skinned hazelnuts can be substituted for the macadamia nuts in the topping.

Serves 12

150g/5oz/1¼ cups plain
   (all-purpose) flour
2.5ml/½ tsp baking powder
a pinch of salt
175g/6oz fine quality white
   chocolate, chopped
90g/3½oz/½ cup caster
   (superfine) sugar

115g/4oz/½ cup unsalted
   (sweet) butter, cut into pieces
2 eggs, lightly beaten
5ml/1 tsp vanilla extract
175g/6oz/1 cup plain (semisweet)
   chocolate chips

For the topping

200g/7oz milk chocolate,
   chopped
215g/7½oz/1⅓ cups unsalted
   macadamia nuts, chopped

1 Preheat the oven to 180°C/350°F/Gas 4. Grease a 23cm/9in springform tin (pan). Sift together the flour, baking powder and salt, and set aside.

2 In a medium pan over a medium heat, melt the white chocolate, sugar and butter until smooth, stirring frequently. Cool slightly, then beat in the eggs and vanilla. Stir in the chocolate chips. Spread evenly in the prepared tin, smoothing the top.

3 Bake for 20–25 minutes, or until a cocktail stick (toothpick) inserted 5cm/2in from the side of the tin comes out clean. Remove from the oven to a heatproof surface, sprinkle chopped milk chocolate over the surface (avoid touching the side of tin) and return to the oven for 1 minute.

4 Remove from the oven and, using the back of a spoon, gently spread out the softened chocolate. Sprinkle with the macadamia nuts and gently press into the chocolate. Cool on a wire rack for 30 minutes, and then chill for 1 hour.

5 Run a sharp knife around the side of the tin to loosen, then unclip and remove. Cut the brownies into thin wedges to serve.

Energy 526kcal/2190kJ; Fat 37.4g, Saturated Fat 16.1g; Carbohydrate 43.8g, Fibre 2.1g

Maple and Pecan Nut Brownies

This recipe provides a delicious adaptation of the classic American chocolate brownie.

115g/4oz/1 cup self-raising
   (self-rising) flour
75g/3oz/½ cup pecan
   nuts, chopped

Makes 12

115g/4oz/½ cup butter, melted
75g/3oz/scant ½ cup soft light
   brown sugar
90ml/6 tbsp maple syrup
2 eggs

For the topping

115g/4oz/⅔ cup plain
   (semisweet) chocolate chips
50g/2oz/¼ cup unsalted
   (sweet) butter
12 pecan nut halves, to decorate

1 Preheat the oven to 180°C/350°F/Gas 4. Line and grease a 25 x 18cm/10 x 7in cake tin (pan).

2 Beat together the melted butter, sugar, 60ml/4 tbsp of the maple syrup, the eggs and flour for 1 minute, or until smooth.

3 Stir in the nuts and transfer to the cake tin. Smooth the surface and bake for 30 minutes, or until risen and firm to the touch. Cool in the tin for 10 minutes, then transfer to a wire rack to cool completely.

4 Melt the chocolate chips, butter and remaining syrup over a low heat. Cool slightly, then spread over the cake. Press in the pecan nut halves, leave to set for about 5 minutes, then cut into squares or bars.

> **Cook's Tips**
> • Maple syrup is a sweet sugar syrup made from the sap of the sugar maple tree. It has a distinctive flavour which is delightful in a variety of sweet recipes as well as being added to ice creams and waffles.
> • Buy a good quality maple syrup as blends are often disappointing.
> • Store opened maple syrup in the refrigerator, as its delicate flavour will deteriorate once the bottle is opened.

Energy 285kcal/1189kJ; Fat 19.4g, Saturated Fat 9.4g; Carbohydrate 26.2g, Fibre 0.8g

American Chocolate Fudge Brownies

This is the classic American recipe, but omit the frosting if you find it too rich.

Makes 12
175g/6oz/³/₄ cup butter
40g/1¹/₂oz/¹/₃ cup unsweetened
   cocoa powder
2 eggs, lightly beaten
175g/6oz/1 cup soft light
   brown sugar

2.5ml/¹/₂ tsp vanilla extract
115g/4oz/1 cup chopped
   pecan nuts
50g/2oz/¹/₂ cup self-raising
   (self-rising) flour

For the frosting
115g/4oz plain
   (semisweet) chocolate
25g/1oz/2 tbsp butter
15ml/1 tbsp sour cream

1 Preheat the oven to 180°C/350°F/Gas 4. Grease a 20cm/8in square shallow cake tin (pan) and line with baking parchment. Melt the butter in a pan and stir in the unsweetened cocoa powder. Set aside to cool.

2 Beat together the eggs, sugar and vanilla extract in a bowl, then stir in the cooled cocoa mixture with the nuts. Sift over the flour and fold into the mixture with a metal spoon.

3 Pour the mixture into the cake tin and bake in the oven for 30–35 minutes, or until risen. Remove from the oven (the mixture will still be quite soft and wet, but it firms up further while cooling) and leave to cool in the tin.

4 To make the frosting, melt the chocolate and butter together in a pan and remove from the heat. Beat in the sour cream until smooth and glossy. Leave to cool slightly, and then spread over the top of the brownies. When set, cut into 12 pieces.

Cook's Tip
Brownies are firm family favourites and, once you find a favourite recipe, you will want to make them regularly. For brownie enthusiasts you can now buy a special pan with a slide-out base, which makes removing the cooked brownies so much easier.

Fudge-glazed Chocolate Brownies

These pecan nut-topped brownies are irresistible, so hide them from friends!

Makes 16
250g/9oz dark (bittersweet)
   chocolate, chopped
25g/1oz unsweetened
   chocolate, chopped
115g/4oz/¹/₂ cup unsalted
   (sweet) butter, cut
   into pieces
90g/3¹/₂oz/scant ¹/₂ cup soft light
   brown sugar
50g/2oz/¹/₄ cup caster
   (superfine) sugar
2 eggs
15ml/1 tbsp vanilla extract

65g/2¹/₂oz/9 tbsp plain
   (all-purpose) flour
115g/4oz/²/₃ cup pecan nuts or
   walnuts, toasted and chopped
150g/5oz white chocolate,
   chopped
pecan nut halves, to decorate
   (optional)

For the glaze
175g/6oz dark (bittersweet)
   chocolate, chopped
50g/2oz/¹/₄ cup unsalted (sweet)
   butter, cut into pieces
30ml/2 tbsp golden (light
   corn) syrup
10ml/2 tsp vanilla extract
5ml/1 tsp instant coffee

1 Preheat oven to 180°C/350°F/Gas 4. Line a 20cm/8in square baking tin (pan) with foil then grease the foil.

2 Melt the dark chocolates and butter in a pan over a low heat. Off the heat, add the sugars and stir for 2 minutes. Beat in the eggs and vanilla extract, and then blend in the flour.

3 Stir in the pecan nuts or walnuts and the chopped white chocolate.

4 Pour into the tin. Bake for 20–25 minutes. Cool in the tin for 30 minutes then lift, using the foil, on to a wire rack to cool for 2 hours.

5 To make the glaze, melt the chocolate in a pan with the butter, golden syrup, vanilla extract and instant coffee. Stir until smooth. Chill the glaze for 1 hour then spread over the brownies. Top with pecan nut halves, if you like. Chill until set then cut into bars.

Energy 335kcal/1396kJ; Fat 25.1g, Saturated fat 11.7g; Carbohydrate 25.6g; Fibre 1.2g

Energy 382kcal/1595kJ; Fat 25g, Saturated fat 12.4g; Carbohydrate 37.6g; Fibre 1.2g

Chocolate Chip Brownies

A double dose of chocolate is incorporated into these melt-in-the-mouth brownies.

Makes 24
115g/4oz plain (semisweet) chocolate
115g/4oz/½ cup butter
3 eggs
200g/7oz/1 cup caster (superfine) sugar
2.5ml/½ tsp vanilla extract
a pinch of salt
150g/5oz/1¼ cups plain (all-purpose) flour
175g/6oz/1 cup chocolate chips

1 Preheat the oven to 180°C/350°F/Gas 4. Then line a 33 x 23cm/13 x 9in baking tin (pan) with baking parchment and grease the paper.

2 Melt the chocolate and butter together in the top of a double boiler, or in a heatproof bowl set over a pan of gently simmering water.

3 Beat together the eggs, sugar, vanilla extract and salt. Stir in the chocolate mixture. Sift over the flour and fold in. Add the chocolate chips.

4 Pour the mixture into the baking tin and spread evenly. Bake until just set, about 30 minutes. The brownies should be slightly moist inside. Leave to cool in the tin.

5 To turn out, run a knife all around the edge and invert on to a baking sheet. Remove the paper. Place another sheet on top and invert again. Cut into bars for serving.

Variations
Rich chocolate: use best quality chocolate (at least 70 per cent cocoa solids) cut into chunks to give the brownies a fantastic flavour.
Chunky choc and nut: use 75g/3oz coarsely chopped white chocolate and 75g/3oz/¾ cup chopped walnuts.
Almond: use almond extract, add 75g/3oz/¾ cup chopped almonds and reduce the chocolate chips to 75g/3oz/½ cup.

Energy 161kcal/674kJ; Fat 8.1g, Saturated fat 4.7g; Carbohydrate 21.3g; Fibre 0.5g

Marbled Brownies

These fancy brownies have an impressive flavour as well as appearance.

Makes 24
225g/8oz plain (semisweet) chocolate
75g/3oz/6 tbsp butter
4 eggs
300g/11oz/1½ cups caster (superfine) sugar
150g/5oz/1¼ cups plain (all-purpose) flour
2.5ml/½ tsp salt
5ml/1 tsp baking powder
10ml/2 tsp vanilla extract
115g/4oz/1 cup chopped walnuts

For the plain mixture
50g/2oz/¼ cup butter, at room temperature
175g/6oz/¾ cup cream cheese
90g/3½oz/1½ cups caster (superfine) sugar
2 eggs
25g/1oz/¼ cup plain (all-purpose) flour
5ml/1 tsp vanilla extract

1 Preheat the oven to 180°C/350°F/Gas 4. Line a 33 x 23cm/ 13 x 9in baking tin (pan) with baking parchment and grease.

2 Melt the chocolate and butter in a small pan over a very low heat, stirring. Set aside to cool. Meanwhile, beat the eggs until light and fluffy. Gradually beat in the sugar. Sift over the flour, salt and baking powder, and fold to combine.

3 Stir in the cooled chocolate mixture. Add the vanilla extract and chopped walnuts. Measure and set aside 475ml/16fl oz/ 2 cups of the chocolate mixture.

4 For the plain mixture, cream the butter and cream cheese with an electric mixer. Add the sugar and continue beating until blended. Beat in the eggs, flour and vanilla extract.

5 Spread the unmeasured chocolate mixture in the tin. Pour over the plain mixture. Drop spoonfuls of the reserved chocolate mixture on top.

6 With a metal spatula, swirl the mixtures to marble them. Do not blend completely. Bake until just set, 35–40 minutes. Turn out when cool and cut into squares for serving.

Energy 259kcal/1083kJ; Fat 15.1g, Saturated fat 7.1g; Carbohydrate 28.8g; Fibre 0.6g

Spice Cake with Ginger Frosting

Preserved stem ginger makes the frosting for this cake particularly delicious.

Makes one 20cm/8in round cake
300ml/10fl oz/1¼ cups milk
30ml/2 tbsp golden (light corn) syrup
10ml/2 tsp vanilla extract
75g/3oz/¾ cup chopped walnuts
175g/6oz/¾ cup butter, at room temperature
285g/10½oz/1½ cups caster (superfine) sugar
1 whole egg, plus 3 egg yolks
275g/10oz/2½ cups plain (all-purpose) flour
15ml/1 tbsp baking powder
5ml/1 tsp freshly grated nutmeg
5ml/1 tsp ground cinnamon
2.5ml/½ tsp ground cloves
1.5ml/¼ tsp ground ginger
1.5ml/¼ tsp mixed (apple pie) spice
preserved stem ginger pieces, to decorate

For the frosting
175g/6oz/¾ cup cream cheese
25g/1oz/2 tbsp unsalted (sweet) butter
200g/7oz/1¾ cups icing (confectioners') sugar
30ml/2 tbsp finely chopped preserved stem ginger
30ml/2 tbsp syrup from stem ginger

1 Preheat the oven to 180°C/350°F/Gas 4. Line and grease three 20cm/8in shallow round cake tins (pans) with baking parchment. In a bowl, combine the milk, golden syrup, vanilla extract and chopped walnuts.

2 Cream the butter and caster sugar until light and fluffy. Beat in the egg and egg yolks.

3 Add the milk and syrup mixture, and stir well. Sift together the flour, baking powder and spices three times. Add to the butter mixture in four batches, folding in carefully.

4 Divide the mixture between the tins. Bake for 25 minutes. Leave in the tins for 5 minutes, then cool on a wire rack.

5 For the frosting, combine the cream cheese with the butter, icing sugar, stem ginger and ginger syrup, beating with a wooden spoon until smooth. Spread the frosting between the layers and over the top. Decorate with pieces of stem ginger.

Energy 5257kcal/21970kJ; Fat 326g, Saturated fat 169.8g; Carbohydrate 572g; Fibre 2.6g

Carrot and Courgette Cake

This unusual sponge has a delicious creamy topping.

Makes one 18cm/7in square cake
1 carrot
1 courgette (zucchini)
3 eggs, separated
115g/4oz/1 cup soft light brown sugar
30ml/2 tbsp ground almonds
finely grated rind of 1 orange
150g/5oz/1¼ cups self-raising (self-rising) wholemeal (whole-wheat) flour
5ml/1 tsp ground cinnamon
5ml/1 tsp icing (confectioners') sugar, for dusting
fondant carrots and courgettes (zucchini), to decorate

For the topping
175g/6oz/¾ cup low-fat soft cheese
5ml/1 tsp clear honey

1 Preheat the oven to 180°C/350°F/Gas 4. Line an 18cm/7in square tin (pan) with baking parchment. Coarsely grate the carrot and courgette.

2 Put the egg yolks, sugar, ground almonds and orange rind into a bowl and whisk until very thick and light. Sift together the flour and cinnamon, and fold into the mixture together with the grated vegetables. Add any bran left in the sieve.

3 Whisk the egg whites until stiff and carefully fold them in, a little at a time. Spoon into the tin. Bake in the oven for 1 hour, covering the top with foil after 40 minutes. Leave to cool in the tin for 5 minutes, then turn out on to a wire rack and remove the lining paper.

4 To make the topping, beat together the cheese and honey, and spread over the cake. Dust with icing sugar and decorate with fondant carrots and courgettes.

> **Cook's Tip**
> To make fondant carrots and courgettes, roll tinted sugarpaste into the shapes and paint details using a fine paintbrush. Use thin lengths of green sugarpaste to make the carrot tops.

Energy 1455kcal/6145kJ; Fat 35g, Saturated fat 14.5g; Carbohydrate 237.8g; Fibre 17.1g

Banana Coconut Cake

Slightly over-ripe bananas are best for this fruity cake topped with honey and coconut.

Makes one 18cm/7in square cake
115g/4oz/1/2 cup butter, softened
115g/4oz/generous 1/2 cup caster (superfine) sugar
2 eggs
115g/4oz/1 cup self-raising (self-rising) flour
50g/2oz/1/2 cup plain (all-purpose) flour
5ml/1 tsp bicarbonate of soda (baking soda)
120ml/4fl oz/1/2 cup milk
2 large bananas, peeled and mashed
75g/3oz/1 cup desiccated (dry unsweetened shredded) coconut, toasted

For the topping
25g/1oz/2 tbsp butter
30ml/2 tbsp clear honey
115g/4oz/2 cups shredded coconut

1 Preheat the oven to 190°C/375°F/Gas 5. Grease a deep 18cm/7in square cake tin (pan), line with baking parchment and grease the paper.

2 Beat the butter and sugar until smooth and creamy. Beat in the eggs, one at a time. Sift together the flours and bicarbonate of soda, sift half into the butter mixture and stir to mix.

3 Combine the milk and mashed banana, and beat half into the egg mixture. Stir in the remaining flour and banana mixtures and the toasted coconut. Transfer the batter to the cake tin and smooth the surface.

4 Bake for 1 hour, or until a skewer inserted into the centre of the cake comes out clean. Leave in the tin for 5 minutes, then turn out on to a wire rack, peel off the paper and leave to cool completely.

5 To make the topping, gently melt the butter and honey in a small pan. Stir in the shredded coconut and cook, stirring, for 5 minutes or until lightly browned. Remove from the heat and allow to cool slightly. Spoon the topping over the cake and allow to cool.

St Clement's Cake

A tangy orange-and-lemon cake makes a spectacular centrepiece when decorated with fruits, silver dragées and fresh flowers.

Makes one 23cm/9in ring cake
175g/6oz/3/4 cup butter
75g/3oz/scant 1/3 cup soft light brown sugar
3 eggs, separated
grated rind and juice of 1 orange
and 1 lemon
150g/5oz/1 1/4 cups self-raising (self-rising) flour
75g/3oz/6 tbsp caster (superfine) sugar
15g/1/2oz/1 tbsp ground almonds
350ml/12fl oz/1 1/2 cups double (heavy) cream
16 crystallized orange and lemon slices, silver dragées, sugared almonds and fresh flowers, to decorate

1 Preheat the oven to 180°C/350°F/Gas 4. Grease and flour a 900ml/1 1/2 pint/3 3/4 cup ring mould.

2 Cream half the butter and all of the brown sugar until pale and light. Beat in the egg yolks, orange rind and juice and fold in 75g/3oz/2/3 cup flour.

3 Cream the remaining butter and the caster sugar in another bowl. Stir in the lemon rind and juice and fold in the remaining flour and the ground almonds. Whisk the egg whites until they form stiff peaks, and fold into the batter.

4 Spoon the two mixtures alternately into the prepared tin. Using a skewer or small spoon, swirl through the mixture to create a marbled effect. Bake for 45–50 minutes, or until risen, and a skewer inserted in the cake comes out clean. Cool in the tin for 10 minutes then transfer to a wire rack to cool.

5 Whip the cream until lightly thickened. Spread over the cooled cake and swirl a pattern over the icing with a metal spatula. Decorate the ring with the crystallized fruits, dragées and sugared almonds to resemble a jewelled crown. Arrange a few fresh flowers with their stems wrapped in foil in the centre.

Energy 3291kcal/13744kJ; Fat 208.5g, Saturated fat 144.6g, Carbohydrate 332.2g; Fibre 24.4g

Energy 4486kcal/18629kJ; Fat 358.8g, Saturated fat 213.6g, Carbohydrate 281.3g; Fibre 5.8g

Apple Cake

A deliciously moist cake with a silky icing.

Makes one ring cake

675g/1½lb apples, peeled, cored
and quartered
500g/1¼lb/generous 4½ cups
caster (superfine) sugar
15ml/1 tbsp water
350g/12oz/3 cups plain
(all-purpose) flour
9ml/1¾ tsp bicarbonate of soda
(baking soda)
5ml/1 tsp ground cinnamon
5ml/1 tsp ground cloves
175g/6oz/generous 1 cup raisins
150g/5oz/1¼ cups
chopped walnuts
225g/8oz/1 cup butter or
margarine, at room temperature
5ml/1 tsp vanilla extract

For the icing

115g/4oz/1 cup icing
(confectioners') sugar
1.5ml/¼ tsp vanilla extract
30–45ml/2–3 tbsp milk

1 Put the apples, 50g/2oz/¼ cup of the sugar and the water in a pan and bring to the boil. Simmer for 25 minutes, stirring occasionally to break up any lumps. Leave to cool. Preheat the oven to 160°C/325°F/Gas 3. Thoroughly butter and flour a 1.75-litre/3-pint/7½-cup tube tin (pan).

2 Sift the flour, bicarbonate of soda and spices into a bowl. Remove 30ml/2 tbsp of the mixture to another bowl and toss with the raisins and 115g/4oz/1 cup of the walnuts.

3 Cream the butter or margarine and remaining sugar together until light and fluffy. Fold in the apple mixture gently. Fold the flour mixture into the apple mixture. Stir in the vanilla extract and the raisin and walnut mixture. Pour into the tube tin. Bake until a skewer inserted in the centre comes out clean, about 1½ hours. Cool completely in the tin on a wire rack, then unmould on to the rack.

4 To make the icing, put the sugar in a bowl and stir in the vanilla extract and 15ml/1 tbsp milk. Add more milk until the icing is smooth and has a thick pouring consistency. Transfer the cake to a serving plate and drizzle the icing over the top. Sprinkle with the remaining nuts. Allow the icing to set.

Energy 7049kcal/29657kJ; Fat 294.1g; Saturated fat 126.6g; Carbohydrate 1103.7g; Fibre 30.4g

Chocolate Marquise

This light-as-air marquise is perfect for sophisticated older children.

Makes one heart-shaped cake

15ml/1 tbsp sunflower oil
75g/3oz/7–8 amaretti, crushed
25g/1oz/2 tbsp unblanched
almonds, toasted and
finely chopped
450g/1lb plain (semisweet)
chocolate, broken into pieces
75ml/5 tbsp golden (light
corn) syrup
475ml/16fl oz/2 cups double
(heavy) cream
cocoa powder, to dust

For the cream

350ml/12fl oz/1½ cups whipping
or double (heavy) cream

1 Lightly oil a 23cm/9in heart-shaped or springform cake tin (pan). Line the base with baking parchment and oil the paper. In a small bowl, combine the crushed amaretti and the toasted and chopped almonds. Sprinkle evenly over the base of the tin.

2 Place the chocolate and golden syrup in a pan over very low heat. Stir frequently until the chocolate is melted and the mixture is smooth. Allow to cool for 6–8 minutes, or until the mixture feels just warm.

3 Beat the cream until it just begins to hold its shape. Stir a large spoonful into the chocolate mixture, then quickly add the remaining cream and gently fold into the chocolate mixture. Pour into the prepared tin and tap the tin gently on the work surface to release any large air bubbles. Cover the tin with clear film (plastic wrap) and leave in the refrigerator overnight.

4 To unmould, run a thin-bladed sharp knife under hot water and dry carefully. Run the knife around the edge of the tin to loosen, place a serving plate over the tin, then invert to unmould. Carefully peel off the paper then dust with cocoa. To make the amaretto cream, whip the cream and serve separately.

Energy 7040kcal/29238kJ; Fat 548.8g; Saturated fat 324.4g; Carbohydrate 448.7g; Fibre 14.2g

Chocolate Cake

This attractive and delicious chocolate cake contains no flour and has a light mousse-like texture.

Makes one 20cm/8in round cake

9 x 25g/1oz squares plain (semisweet) chocolate

175g/6oz/³⁄₄ cup butter, softened
130g/3¹⁄₂oz/²⁄₃ cup caster (superfine) sugar
225g/8oz/2 cups ground almonds
4 eggs, separated
4 x 25g/1oz squares white chocolate, melted, to decorate

1 Preheat the oven to 180°C/350°F/Gas 4. Grease and base-line a 20cm/8in springform cake tin (pan).

2 Melt the chocolate in a heatproof bowl over a pan of simmering water. Beat 115g/4oz/¹⁄₂ cup butter and all the sugar until light and fluffy in a large bowl. Add two-thirds of the plain chocolate, the almonds and egg yolks, and beat well.

3 Whisk the egg whites in another clean, dry bowl until stiff peaks form. Fold them into the chocolate mixture, then transfer to the tin and smooth the surface. Bake for 50–55 minutes, or until a skewer inserted into the centre comes out clean.

4 Cool in the tin for 5 minutes, then remove from the tin and transfer to a wire rack. Remove the lining paper and cool completely.

5 Place the remaining butter and remaining melted chocolate in a pan. Heat very gently, stirring constantly, until melted. Place a large sheet of baking parchment under the wire rack to catch any drips. Pour the chocolate topping over the cake, allowing the topping to coat the top and sides. Leave to set for at least 1 hour.

6 To decorate, fill a paper piping (icing) bag with the melted white chocolate and snip the end. Drizzle the white chocolate around the edges. Use any remaining chocolate to pipe leaves on to baking parchment or greaseproof (waxed) paper. Allow to set then place on top of the cake.

One-stage Chocolate Sponge

For parties, quick and easy favourites like this chocolate cake are invaluable.

Makes one 18cm/7in round cake

175g/6oz/³⁄₄ cup soft margarine, at room temperature
115g/4oz/generous ¹⁄₂ cup caster (superfine) sugar
50g/2oz/4 tbsp golden (light corn) syrup

175g/6oz/1¹⁄₂ cups self-raising (self-rising) flour, sifted
45ml/3 tbsp unsweetened cocoa powder, sifted
2.5ml/¹⁄₂ tsp salt
3 eggs, beaten
a little milk, as required
150ml/¹⁄₄ pint/²⁄₃ cup whipping cream
15–30ml/1–2 tbsp fine shred marmalade
icing (confectioners') sugar, for dusting

1 Preheat the oven to 180°C/350°F/Gas 4. Lightly grease or line two 18cm/7in shallow round cake tins (pans).

2 Place the margarine, sugar, syrup, flour, cocoa powder, salt and eggs in a large bowl, and cream together until well blended using a wooden spoon or electric whisk. If the mixture seems a little thick, stir in 15–30ml/1–2 tbsp milk, until you have a soft dropping consistency.

3 Spoon the mixture into the prepared tins and bake for about 30 minutes, changing shelves if necessary after 15 minutes, until the tops are just firm and the cakes are springy to the touch.

4 Leave the cakes to cool for 5 minutes, then remove from the tins and leave to cool completely on a wire rack.

5 Whip the cream and fold in the marmalade, then use to sandwich the two cakes together. Sprinkle the top with sifted icing sugar.

> **Cook's Tip**
> You could also use butter at room temperature cut into small pieces for this one-stage sponge mixture.

Energy 5162kcal/21484kJ; Fat 385.5g, Saturated fat 163.5g; Carbohydrate 353.6g; Fibre 22.3g

Energy 3476kcal/14495kJ; Fat 234g, Saturated fat 78.4g; Carbohydrate 315.7g; Fibre 10.9g

Chocolate Orange Battenberg Cake

A tasty variation on the traditional pink-and-white Battenberg cake. Use good quality marzipan for the best flavour.

Makes one 18cm/7in long rectangular cake

115g/4oz/½ cup soft margarine
115g/4oz/½ cup caster
  (superfine) sugar
2 eggs, beaten
a few drops of vanilla extract
15g/½oz/1 tbsp ground almonds
115g/4oz/1 cup self-raising
  (self-rising) flour, sifted
grated rind and juice of ½ orange
15g/½oz/2 tbsp unsweetened
  cocoa powder, sifted
30–45ml/2–3 tbsp milk
1 jar chocolate and nut spread
225g/8oz white marzipan

1 Preheat the oven to 180°C/350°F/Gas 4. Grease and line an 18cm/7in square cake tin (pan) with baking parchment. Put a double piece of foil across the middle of the tin, to divide it into two equal oblongs.

2 Cream the margarine and sugar. Beat in the eggs, vanilla extract and almonds. Divide the mixture evenly into two halves.

3 Fold half of the flour into one half, with the orange rind and enough juice to give a soft dropping consistency. Fold the rest of the flour and the cocoa powder into the other half, with enough milk to give a soft dropping consistency. Fill the tin with the two mixes and level the top.

4 Bake for 15 minutes, reduce the heat to 160°C/325°F/Gas 3 and cook for 20–30 minutes, or until the top is just firm. Leave to cool in the tin for a few minutes. Turn out on to a board, cut each cake into two strips and trim evenly. Leave to cool.

5 Using the chocoleate and nut spread, sandwich the cakes together, Battenberg-style.

6 Roll out the marzipan on a board lightly dusted with cornflour to a rectangle 18cm/7in wide and long enough to wrap around the cake. Wrap the paste around the cake, putting the join underneath. Press to seal.

Energy 3916kcal/16370kJ; Fat 234.1g, Saturated fat 41.6g; Carbohydrate 426.6g; Fibre 9.3g

Best-ever Chocolate Sandwich

A three-layered cake is ideal for a birthday party.

Makes one 20cm/8in round cake

115g/4oz/1 cup plain
  (all-purpose) flour
50g/2oz/½ cup unsweetened
  cocoa powder
5ml/1 tsp baking powder
6 eggs
225g/8oz/generous 1 cup caster
  (superfine) sugar

10ml/2 tsp vanilla extract
115g/4oz/½ cup unsalted (sweet)
  butter, melted

For the icing

225g/8oz plain (semisweet)
  chocolate, chopped
75g/3oz/6 tbsp unsalted
  (sweet) butter
3 eggs, separated
250ml/8fl oz/1 cup whipping cream
45ml/3 tbsp caster
  (superfine) sugar

1 Preheat the oven to 180°C/350°F/Gas 4. Line three 20cm/8in round shallow cake tins (pans) with baking parchment, grease the paper and dust with flour. Sift the flour, cocoa powder, baking powder and a pinch of salt together three times.

2 Place the eggs and sugar in the top of a double boiler. Beat until doubled in volume. Add the vanilla extract. Fold in the flour mixture in three batches, then the melted butter. Transfer the mixture into the tins. Bake until the cakes pull away from the tin sides, about 25 minutes. Transfer to a wire rack.

3 To make the icing, melt the chocolate in the top of a double boiler. Off the heat, stir in the butter and egg yolks. Return to the heat and stir until thick. Whip the cream until firm.

4 In another bowl, beat the egg whites until stiff peaks form. Add the sugar and beat until glossy. Fold the cream, then the egg whites, into the chocolate mixture. Chill the cake for 20 minutes, then sandwich together and cover with icing.

Variation
Try coffee butter icing (see p88) instead of chocolate icing.

Energy 5787kcal/24151kJ; Fat 382.2g, Saturated fat 220.4g; Carbohydrate 528g; Fibre 15.2g

One-stage Victoria Sandwich

This recipe can be used as the base for other cakes.

Makes one 18cm/7in round cake

175g/6oz/1½ cups self-raising (self-rising) flour
a pinch of salt
175g/6oz/¾ cup butter, softened
175g/6oz/scant 1 cup caster (superfine) sugar
3 eggs

To finish
60–90ml/4–6 tbsp raspberry jam
caster (superfine) sugar or icing (confectioners') sugar

1 Preheat the oven to 180°C/350°F/Gas 4. Grease two 18cm/7in shallow round cake tins (pans), line the bases with baking parchment and grease the paper.

2 Put the flour, salt, butter, caster sugar and eggs into a large bowl. Whisk the ingredients together until smooth and creamy.

3 Divide the mixture between the prepared cake tins and smooth the surfaces. Bake for 25–30 minutes, or until a skewer inserted into the centre of the cakes comes out clean.

4 Turn out on to a wire rack, peel off the lining paper and leave to cool. Place one of the cakes on a serving plate and spread with the raspberry jam. Place the other cake on top.

5 Cut out paper star shapes, place on the cake and dredge with sugar. Remove the paper to reveal the pattern.

Variation
Sponge Cake with Strawberries and Cream is delicious on a summer's day. Whip 300ml/½ pint/1¼ cups double (heavy) cream with 5ml/1 tsp icing (confectioners') sugar until stiff. Wash and hull 450g/1lb/4 cups strawberries, then cut them in half. Spread one of the cakes with half of the cream and sprinkle over half of the strawberries. Place the other cake on top, spread with the remaining cream and arrange the remaining strawberries.

Energy 2965kcal/12419kJ; Fat 162.8g, Saturated fat 96.2g; Carbohydrate 361.3g; Fibre 5.4g

Mocha Victoria Sponge

A light coffee- and cocoa-flavoured sponge with a rich buttercream topping.

Makes one 18cm/7in round cake
175g/6oz/¾ cup butter
175g/6oz/generous ¾ cup caster (superfine) sugar
3 eggs
175g/6oz/1½ cups self-raising (self-rising) flour, sifted
15ml/1 tbsp strong black coffee
15ml/1 tbsp unsweetened cocoa powder mixed with 15–30ml/1–2 tbsp boiling water

For the coffee buttercream
150g/5oz/10 tbsp butter
15ml/1 tbsp coffee extract or 10ml/2 tsp instant coffee powder dissolved in 15–30ml/1–2 tbsp warm milk
275g/10oz/2½ cups icing (confectioners') sugar

1 Preheat the oven to 180°C/350°F/Gas 4. Grease and base-line two 18cm/7in shallow round cake tins (pans). Cream the butter and sugar in a large bowl until light and fluffy. Add the eggs, one at a time, beating well after each addition. Fold in the flour.

2 Divide the mixture between two bowls. Fold the coffee into one and the cocoa mixture into the other.

3 Place alternate spoonfuls of each mixture side by side in the cake tins. Bake for 25–30 minutes. Turn out on to a wire rack to cool.

4 For the buttercream, beat the butter until soft. Gradually beat in the remaining ingredients until smooth.

5 Sandwich the cakes, bases together, with a third of the buttercream. Cover the top and side with the remainder.

Cook's Tip
When mixing eggs into creamed sugar and butter, whisk only briefly, and if the mixture begins to curdle add a spoonful of the flour before you add any more of the eggs.

Energy 4668kcal/19505kJ; Fat 289.6g, Saturated fat 176.4g; Carbohydrate 506.1g; Fibre 7.2g

Strawberry Shortcake Gateau

A light cookie-textured sponge forms the base of this summertime cake.

Makes one 20cm/8in round cake

225g/8oz/2 cups fresh strawberries, hulled
30ml/2 tbsp orange juice
225g/8oz/2 cups self-raising (self-rising) flour
10ml/2 tsp baking powder
75g/3oz/6 tbsp unsalted (sweet) butter, diced
40g/1½oz/3 tbsp caster (superfine) sugar
1 egg, lightly beaten
15–30ml/1–2 tbsp milk
melted butter, for brushing
250ml/8fl oz/1 cup double (heavy) cream
icing (confectioners') sugar, for dusting

1 Preheat the oven to 220°C/425°F/Gas 7. Grease and base-line two 20cm/8in shallow, round, loose-based cake tins (pans).

2 Reserve 5 strawberries, slice the remainder and marinate in the orange juice for about 1–2 hours. Strain, reserving the juice.

3 Sift the flour and baking powder into a bowl. Rub in the butter until the mixture resembles fine breadcrumbs and stir in the sugar. Work in the egg and 15ml/1 tbsp of the milk to form a soft dough, adding more milk if needed.

4 Knead briefly on a lightly floured surface and divide into two pieces. Roll out each piece, mark one into eight wedges, and transfer both to the prepared cake tins. Brush with a little melted butter and bake for 15 minutes. Cool in the tins for 10 minutes, then transfer to a wire rack to cool completely.

5 Cut the marked cake into wedges. Reserving a little cream for decoration, whip the remainder until it holds its shape, and fold in the reserved juice and marinated strawberry slices. Spread over the round cake. Place the wedges on top tilting them at a slight angle, and dust with icing sugar.

6 Whip the remaining cream and use to pipe swirls on each wedge. Halve the reserved strawberries and decorate the cake.

Almond and Raspberry Roll

A light and airy sponge cake is rolled up with a fresh cream and raspberry filling for a delightful treat.

Makes one 23cm/9in long roll

3 eggs
75g/3oz/6 tbsp caster (superfine) sugar
50g/2oz/½ cup plain (all-purpose) flour
30ml/2 tbsp ground almonds
caster (superfine) sugar, for dusting
250ml/8fl oz/1 cup double (heavy) cream
225g/8oz/1⅓ cups fresh raspberries
16 flaked almonds, toasted, to decorate

1 Preheat the oven to 200°C/400°F/Gas 6. Grease a 33 x 23cm/13 x 9in Swiss roll tin (jelly roll pan) and line with baking parchment. Grease the paper.

2 Whisk the eggs and sugar in a heatproof bowl until blended. Place the bowl over a pan of simmering water and whisk until thick and pale.

3 Whisk off the heat until cool. Sift over the flour and almonds, and fold in gently.

4 Transfer to the prepared tin and bake for 10–12 minutes, until risen and springy to the touch.

5 Invert the cake in its tin on to baking parchment dusted with caster sugar. Leave to cool, then remove the tin and lining paper.

6 Reserve a little cream, then whip the remainder until it holds its shape. Fold in all but 8 raspberries and spread the mixture over the cooled cake, leaving a narrow border. Roll the cake up and sprinkle with caster sugar.

7 Whip the reserved cream until it just holds its shape, and spoon or pipe a line along the top of the roll in the centre. Decorate the cream with the reserved raspberries and toasted flaked almonds.

Energy 2911kcal/12118kJ; Fat 204.9g, Saturated fat 124.7g; Carbohydrate 239.1g; Fibre 9.4g

Energy 2166kcal/9012kJ; Fat 169g, Saturated fat 89.8g; Carbohydrate 133.9g; Fibre 9.4g

Orange and Walnut Swiss Roll

This unusual cake is tasty enough to serve alone, but you could also pour over some single (light) cream.

Makes one 23cm/9in long roll
4 eggs, separated
115g/4oz/generous ½ cup caster (superfine) sugar
115g/4oz/1 cup very finely chopped walnuts
a pinch of cream of tartar
a pinch of salt
icing (confectioners') sugar, for dusting

For the filling
300ml/½ pint/1¼ cups whipping cream
15ml/1 tbsp caster (superfine) sugar
grated rind of 1 orange

1 Preheat the oven to 180°C/350°F/Gas 4. Line a 30 × 23cm/ 12 × 9in Swiss roll tin (jelly roll pan) with baking parchment and grease the paper.

2 Beat the egg yolks and sugar until thick. Stir in the walnuts. In another bowl beat the egg whites with the cream of tartar and salt until stiffly peaking. Fold into the walnut mixture.

3 Pour the mixture into the prepared tin and level the top. Bake for 15 minutes. Invert the cake on to baking parchment dusted with icing sugar. Peel off the lining paper. Roll up the cake with the sugared paper. Leave to cool.

4 For the filling, whip the cream until softly peaking. Fold in the caster sugar and orange rind.

5 Unroll the cake. Spread with the filling, then re-roll. Chill. To serve, dust with icing sugar.

Cook's Tip
Rolling up the Swiss roll (jelly roll) while still warm ensures that it will re-roll around its cream filling when it is cold without cracking.

Chocolate Roll

Fresh cream in a chocolate roll is always popular.

Makes one 33cm/13in long roll
225g/8oz plain (semisweet) chocolate
45ml/3 tbsp water
30ml/2 tbsp strong coffee
7 eggs, separated
175g/6oz/scant 1 cup caster (superfine) sugar
1.5ml/¼ tsp salt
icing (confectioners') sugar, for dusting
350ml/12fl oz/1½ cups whipping cream

1 Preheat the oven to 180°C/350°F/Gas 4. Line and grease a 38 × 33cm/15 × 13in Swiss roll tin (jelly roll pan) with baking parchment. Combine the chocolate, water and coffee in the top of a double boiler or in a heatproof bowl over a pan of simmering water. Heat until melted. Set aside.

2 With an electric mixer, beat the egg yolks and sugar until thick. Stir in the melted chocolate. In another bowl, beat the egg whites and salt until they hold stiff peaks. Fold a large dollop of egg whites into the yolk mixture to lighten it, then carefully fold in the rest of the egg whites.

3 Pour the mixture into the tin and smooth evenly with a metal spatula. Bake for 15 minutes. Remove from the oven, cover with baking parchment and a damp cloth. Leave to stand for 1–2 hours. With an electric mixer, whip the cream until stiff. Set aside.

4 Run a knife along the inside edge of the tin to loosen the cake, then invert the cake on to a sheet of baking parchment that has been dusted with icing sugar.

5 Whip the cream until it holds its shape. Peel off the lining paper. Spread with an even layer of whipped cream, then roll up the cake using the sugared paper.

6 Chill for several hours. Before serving, dust with an even layer of icing sugar.

Fruit Salad Cake

You can use any combination of dried fruits in this rich, dark fruit cake.

Makes one 18cm/7in round cake
175g/6oz/1 cup roughly chopped
    mixed dried fruit, such as
    apples, apricots, prunes
    and peaches
250ml/8fl oz/1 cup hot tea

225g/8oz/2 cups self-raising
    (self-rising) wholemeal
    (whole-wheat) flour
5ml/1 tsp freshly grated nutmeg
50g/2oz/¼ cup muscovado
    (molasses) sugar
45ml/3 tbsp sunflower oil
45ml/3 tbsp skimmed milk
demerara (raw) sugar,
    for sprinkling

1 Soak the dried fruits in the tea for several hours or overnight. Drain and reserve the liquid.

2 Preheat the oven to 180°C/350°F/Gas 4. Grease an 18cm/7in round cake tin (pan) and line the base with baking parchment.

3 Sift the flour into a bowl with the nutmeg. Stir in the muscovado sugar, and the dried fruit and tea. Add the oil and milk, and mix well.

4 Spoon the mixture into the prepared cake tin and sprinkle with demerara sugar.

5 Bake for 50–55 minutes, or until firm. Turn out on to a wire rack to cool.

Cook's Tips
• *For successful baking always level the mixture in the cake tin (pan) before baking.*
• *Test that the cake is cooked before the stated cooking time as oven temperatures can vary and it might take less time. Fan-assisted ovens usually cook foods more quickly.*
• *Check that the oven shelf is level, as an uneven surface will cause the cake to cook lopsidedly.*

Energy 1482kcal/6266kJ; Fat 39.1g, Saturated fat 4.7g; Carbohydrate 261.9g; Fibre 31.3g

Fairy Cakes with Blueberries

This luxurious treatment of fairy cakes means they will be as popular with adults as with children.

Makes 8–10
115g/4oz/½ cup soft margarine
115g/4oz/½ cup caster
    (superfine) sugar
5ml/1 tsp grated lemon rind

a pinch of salt
2 eggs, beaten
115g/4oz/1 cup self-raising
    (self-rising) flour, sifted
120ml/4fl oz/½ cup
    whipping cream
75–115g/3–4oz/¾–1 cup
    blueberries
icing (confectioners') sugar,
    for dusting

1 Preheat the oven to 190°C/375°F/Gas 5. Cream the margarine, sugar, lemon rind and salt in a large bowl until pale and fluffy.

2 Gradually beat in the eggs, then fold in the flour.

3 Spoon the mixture into eight to ten paper cases on baking sheets and bake for 15–20 minutes, or until just golden.

4 Leave the cakes to cool, then scoop out a circle of sponge from the top of each using the point of a small sharp knife, and set them aside.

5 Whip the cream and place a spoonful in each cake, plus a couple of blueberries. Replace the lids at an angle and sift over some icing sugar.

Variation
These fairy cakes are perfect for making into Angel Cakes with butter icing. Slice the domed top from the cake and cut in two. Make some butter icing and flavour it as you like (orange or chocolate are particular favourites with children). Spread some butter icing on the top of each cake and position the cut tops with the cut sides outwards to look like wings.

Energy 231kcal/962kJ; Fat 15.5g, Saturated fat 3.4g; Carbohydrate 21.5g; Fibre 0.6g

Chocolate Fairy Cakes

These fairy cakes have a rich butter icing that children will love.

Makes 24
115g/4oz good quality plain
 (semi-sweet) chocolate, cut
 into small pieces
15ml/1 tbsp water
300g/10oz/2½ cups plain
 (all-purpose) flour
5ml/1 tsp baking powder
2.5ml/½ tsp bicarbonate of soda
 (baking soda)
a pinch of salt
300g/11oz/generous 1½ cups
 caster (superfine) sugar
175g/6oz/¾ cup butter or
 margarine, at room temperature
150ml/¼ pint/⅔ cup milk
5ml/1 tsp vanilla extract
3 eggs
1 recipe quantity butter icing,
 flavoured to taste, see p88

1 Preheat the oven to 180°C/350°F/Gas 4. Grease and flour 24 deep bun cups, about 6.5cm/2¾in in diameter, or use paper cases in the tins (pans).

2 Put the chocolate and water in a bowl set over a pan of almost simmering water. Heat until melted and smooth, stirring. Remove from the heat and leave to cool.

3 Sift the flour, baking powder, bicarbonate of soda, salt and sugar into a large bowl. Add the chocolate mixture, butter or margarine, milk and vanilla extract.

4 With an electric mixer on medium-low speed, beat until smoothly blended. Increase the speed to high and beat for 2 minutes. Add the eggs and beat for 2 more minutes.

5 Divide the mixture evenly among the prepared bun tins and bake for 20–25 minutes, or until a skewer inserted into the centre of a cake comes out clean.

6 Cool in the tins for 10 minutes, then turn out to cool completely on a wire rack.

7 Ice the top of each cake with butter icing, swirling it into a peak in the centre.

Energy 228kcal/957kJ; Fat 11.5g, Saturated fat 3.3g; Carbohydrate 30.6g; Fibre 0.5g

Chocolate Mint-filled Cupcakes

For extra mint flavour, chop eight thin mint cream-filled after-dinner mints and fold into the cake batter.

Makes 12
225g/8oz/2 cups plain
 (all-purpose) flour
5ml/1 tsp bicarbonate of soda
 (baking soda)
a pinch of salt
50g/2oz/½ cup unsweetened
 cocoa powder
150g/5oz/10 tbsp unsalted
 (sweet) butter, softened
300g/11oz/generous 1½ cups
 caster (superfine) sugar
3 eggs
5ml/1 tsp peppermint extract
250ml/8fl oz/1 cup milk

For the filling
300ml/½ pint/1¼ cups double
 (heavy) or whipping cream
5ml/1 tsp peppermint extract

For the glaze
175g/6oz plain
 (semisweet) chocolate
115g/4oz/½ cup unsalted
 (sweet) butter
5ml/1 tsp peppermint extract

1 Preheat the oven to 180°C/350°F/Gas 4. Line a 12-cup bun tray with paper cases. Sift together the dry ingredients.

2 In another bowl, beat the butter and sugar until light and creamy. Add the eggs, one at a time, beating well after each addition; beat in the peppermint. On low speed, beat in the flour mixture alternately with the milk, until just blended. Spoon into the paper cases.

3 Bake for 12–15 minutes. Transfer to a wire rack to cool. When cool, remove the paper cases.

4 To make the filling, whip the cream and peppermint extract until stiff. Spoon into a piping (icing) bag fitted with a small plain nozzle. Pipe 15ml/1 tbsp into each cake through the base.

5 To make the glaze, melt the chocolate and butter in a heatproof bowl over a pan of simmering water, stirring until smooth. Remove from the heat and stir in the peppermint extract. Cool, then spread on top of each cake.

Energy 535kcal/2234kJ; Fat 35.1g, Saturated fat 21.4g; Carbohydrate 52g; Fibre 1.4g

Ghost Cake

This children's cake is really simple to make yet very effective. It is ideal for a Halloween party.

Serves 15–20
900g/2lb/6 cups white
   sugarpaste icing
black food colouring

2 Madeira cakes, baked in an
   18cm/7in square cake tin and
   a 300ml/½ pint/1¼ cup
   pudding bowl
350g/12oz/1½ cups butter icing

Materials/equipment
23cm/9in round cake board
fine paintbrush

1 Tint 115g/4oz/¾ cup of the sugarpaste icing dark grey and use to cover the cake board.

2 Cut two small corners off the large cake. Cut two larger wedges off the other two corners, then stand the cake on the board. Divide the larger trimmings in half and wedge around the base of the cake.

3 Secure the small cake to the top of the larger cake with butter icing. Completely cover both of the cakes with the remaining butter icing.

4 Roll out the remaining sugarpaste icing to an oval shape 50 × 30cm/20 × 12in. Lay it over the cake, letting the icing fall into folds around the sides.

5 Gently smooth the icing over the top half of the cake using your hands, and trim off any excess sugarpaste.

6 Using black food colouring and a fine paintbrush, paint two oval eyes on to the head.

Cook's Tip

Instead of painting on the eyes you could colour some sugarpaste trimmings black and cut out two ovals using a small oval cutter, if you like.

Cat-in-a-Basket Cake

This adorable cat, asleep in its basket, will appeal to all children.

Makes one 15cm/6in round cake
800g/1¾lb marzipan
red, green, yellow and brown
   food colouring
15cm/6in round deep
   sponge cake

30ml/2 tbsp apricot jam, warmed
   and sieved
50g/2oz/4 tbsp white
   sugarpaste icing

Materials/equipment
20cm/8in round cake board
fine paintbrush

1 Tint 350g/12oz/2¼ cups of the marzipan pink. Divide the rest in half and tint one half green and the other yellow. Brush the cake with the apricot jam and place it on the board.

2 Roll out the pink marzipan to a rectangle measuring 15 × 25cm/6 × 10in. Cut five 1cm/½in wide strips, about 24cm/9½in long, keeping them attached to the rectangle at one end.

3 Roll out the green marzipan and cut it into 7.5cm/3in lengths of the same width. Fold back alternate pink strips and lay a green strip across widthways. Bring the pink strips over the green strip to form the weave. Keep repeating the process until the entire length is woven. Press lightly to join. Repeat with the rest of the rectangle and more strips of green marzipan.

4 Press the two pieces of basketweave on to the side of the cake, joining them neatly. Model a yellow marzipan cat about 7.5cm/3in across. Leave to dry overnight.

5 Roll out the sugarpaste icing and place on the centre of the cake. Put the cat on top and arrange the icing in folds around it. Trim the edges neatly.

6 Make long ropes from any leftover pink and green marzipan. Twist together and press on to the top edge of the cake. Paint the cat's features in brown food colouring.

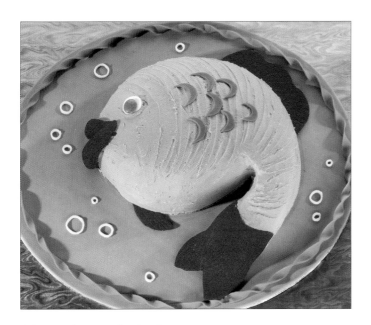

Fish-shaped Cake

A very easy and colourful cake, this fun little fish is perfect for a small child's birthday party.

Makes one cake
450g/1lb/3 cups sugarpaste icing
blue, orange, red, mauve and
    green food colouring
sponge cake, baked in a 3.5 litre/
    6 pint/15 cup ovenproof
    mixing bowl
350g/12oz/1½ cups butter icing
1 blue sweet (candy)

Materials/equipment
large oval cake board
2.5cm/1in plain cutter
baking parchment piping
    (icing) bag

1 Tint two-thirds of the sugarpaste icing blue, roll out very thinly and use to cover the dampened cake board.

2 Make a template of a fish out of paper. Invert the cake, place the template on top and trim into the fish shape. Slope the sides. Place on the cake board.

3 Tint all but 15ml/1 tbsp of the butter icing orange. Use to cover the cake, smoothing with a metal spatula. Score curved lines for scales, starting from the tail end.

4 Tint half the remaining sugarpaste icing red. Shape and position two lips.

5 Cut out the tail and fins. Mark with lines using a knife and position on the fish. Make the eye from white sugarpaste and the blue sweet.

6 Tint a little sugarpaste mauve, cut out crescent-shaped scales using a biscuit cutter and place on the fish. Tint the remaining sugarpaste green and cut into long thin strips. Twist each strip and arrange around the board.

7 To make the bubbles around the fish, place the reserved butter icing in a piping bag, snip off the end and pipe small circles on to the board.

Energy 5866kcal/24548kJ; Fat 327.6g, Saturated fat 139g; Carbohydrate 733.6g; Fibre 5.4g

Pink Monkey Cake

This cheeky little monkey could be made in any colour icing you wish.

Makes one 20cm/8in cake
20cm/8in round sponge cake
115g/4oz/½ cup butter icing
45ml/3 tbsp apricot jam, warmed
    and sieved
450g/1lb marzipan
500g/1¼lb/3¾ cups
    sugarpaste icing
    red, blue and black
    food colouring

Materials/equipment
25cm/10in round cake board
2 candles and holders

1 Trace the outline and paws of the monkey from the photograph. Using a photocopier or a computer enlarge to fit the cake and then cut out a template.

2 Split the cake and fill with butter icing. Place on the cake board and use the template to cut out the basic shape of the monkey. Use the trimmings to shape the nose and tummy. Brush with apricot jam and cover with a layer of marzipan.

3 Tint 450g/1lb/3 cups of the sugarpaste icing pale pink and use to cover the cake. Leave to dry overnight.

4 Mark the position of the face and paws. Tint a little of the sugarpaste icing blue and use for the eyes. Tint a little icing black and cut out the pupils and tie.

5 Tint the remaining sugarpaste icing dark pink and cut out the nose, mouth, ears and paws. Stick all the features in place with water. Roll the trimmings into balls and place on the board to hold the candles.

Variation
You could adapt this circular cake to make a cat or an elephant, perhaps side on with his trunk curling upwards. Try some different shapes on paper then transfer your finished idea on to baking parchment to use as a template.

Energy 6888kcal/28960kJ; Fat 288.6g, Saturated fat 71.3g; Carbohydrate 1068.1g; Fibre 14.9g

Porcupine Cake

Melt-in-the-mouth pieces of flaked chocolate give this porcupine its spiky coating.

Serves 15–20
2 chocolate sponge cakes, baked in a 1.2 litre/2 pint/5 cup and a 600ml/1 pint/2½ cup pudding bowl
500g/1¼lb/2½ cups chocolate-flavour butter icing

cream, black, green, brown and red food colouring
5–6 flaked chocolate bars
50g/2oz/⅓ cup white marzipan

Materials/equipment
35cm/14in long rectangular cake board
wooden cocktail stick (toothpick)
fine paintbrush

1 Use the smaller cake for the head and shape a pointed nose at one end. Reserve the trimmed wedges.

2 Place the cakes side-by-side on the cake board, inverted, and use the trimmings to fill in the sides and top where they meet. Secure with butter icing.

3 Cover the cake with the remaining butter icing and mark the nose with a cocktail stick.

4 Make the spikes by breaking the flaked chocolate into thin strips and sticking them into the butter icing all over the body section of the porcupine.

5 Reserve a small portion of marzipan. Divide the remainder into three and tint cream, black and green.

6 Tint a tiny portion of the reserved marzipan brown.

7 Shape cream ears and feet, black-and-white eyes, and black claws and nose. Arrange all the features on the cake and press them into the buttercream.

8 Make green apples and highlight in red with a fine paintbrush. Make the stalks from the brown marzipan and push them in to the apples.

Energy 364kcal/1523kJ; Fat 22.4g, Saturated fat 5.7g; Carbohydrate 39g; Fibre 0.1g

Mouse-in-Bed Cake

This cake is suitable for both girls and boys. Make the mouse well in advance to give it time to dry.

Makes one 20 x 15cm/ 8 x 6in cake
20cm/8in square sponge cake
115g/4oz/½ cup butter icing
45ml/3 tbsp apricot jam, warmed and sieved

450g/1lb marzipan
675g/1½lb/4½ cups sugarpaste icing
blue and red food colouring

Materials/equipment
25cm/10in square cake board
flower cutter
blue and red food colouring pens

1 Cut 5cm/2in off one side of the cake. Split and fill the main cake with butter icing. Place on the cake board, brush with apricot jam and cover with a layer of marzipan.

2 With the cake off-cut, shape a pillow with a hollow for the mouse's head, and the torso and the legs of the mouse. Cover with marzipan and leave to dry overnight.

3 Cover the cake and pillow with white sugarpaste icing. Lightly frill the edge of the pillow with a fork. To make the valance, roll out 350g/12oz/2¼ cups of sugarpaste icing and cut into four 7.5cm/3in wide strips. Attach to the bed with water. Arrange the pillow and mouse body on the cake.

4 For the quilt, tint 75g/3oz/½ cup of sugarpaste icing blue and roll out to an 18cm/7in square. Mark with a diamond pattern and the flower cutter. Cover the mouse with the quilt.

5 Cut a 2.5 x 19cm/1 x 7½in white sugarpaste icing strip for the sheet, mark the edge and place over the quilt, tucking it under at the top edge.

6 Tint 25g/1oz/2 tbsp of marzipan pink and make the head and paws of the mouse. Put the head on the pillow, tucked under the sheet, and the paws over the edge of the sheet. Use food colouring pens to draw on the face of the mouse.

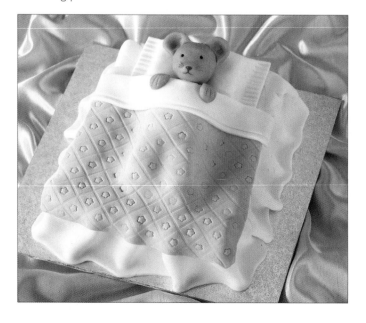

Energy 7749kcal/32592kJ; Fat 315.8g, Saturated fat 77.1g; Carbohydrate 1225g; Fibre 15.8g

Teddy's Birthday

After the sugarpaste pieces have been assembled and stuck into the cake, an icing smoother is useful to flatten the design.

Makes one 20cm/8in round cake

20cm/8in round cake
115g/4oz/½ cup butter icing
45ml/3 tbsp apricot jam, warmed and sieved
350g/12oz marzipan
450g/1lb/3 cups sugarpaste icing
brown, red, blue and black food colouring
115g/4oz/¾ cup royal icing
edible silver balls

Materials/equipment

25cm/10in round cake board
small baking parchment piping (icing) bags
medium shell and star nozzles
1.5m/1½yd red ribbon
2 candles and holders

1 Copy the teddy design on to a piece of paper that will fit the top of the cake.

2 Split the cake and fill with butter icing. Place on the cake board and brush with apricot jam. Cover with a layer of marzipan then a layer of sugarpaste icing.

3 Using the paper template, mark the design on top of the cake.

4 Colour one-third of the remaining sugarpaste icing pale brown. Colour a piece pink, a piece red, some blue and a tiny piece black. Using the template, cut out the pieces and place in position on the cake. Stick down by lifting the edges carefully and brushing the undersides with a little water.

5 Roll small ovals for the eyes and stick in place with the nose and eyebrows. Cut out a mouth and press flat.

6 Tie the ribbon around the cake. Colour the royal icing blue and pipe the border around the base of the cake with the shell nozzle. Pipe tiny stars around the small cake with the star nozzle. Insert silver balls on the piped stars. Put the candles on the cake.

Energy 6210kcal/26127kJ; Fat 248.8g, Saturated fat 64.5g; Carbohydrate 995.4g; Fibre 12.1g

Party Teddy Bear Cake

The cuddly teddy on this cake is built up with royal icing and coloured coconut and is a very simple effect to achieve.

Makes one 20cm/8in square cake

20cm/8in square sponge cake
115g/4oz/½ cup butter icing
45ml/3 tbsp apricot jam, warmed and sieved
450g/1lb marzipan
350g/12oz/2¼ cups white sugarpaste icing
25g/1oz/⅓ cup desiccated (dry unsweetened shredded) coconut
blue and black food colouring
115g/4oz/¾ cup royal icing

Materials/equipment

25cm/10in square cake board
2 small baking parchment piping (icing) bags
small red bow
no.7 shell nozzle
1.5m/1½yd red ribbon
6 candles and holders

1 Make a paper template of the teddy so that it will fit the top of the cake.

2 Cut the cake in half and sandwich together with butter icing. Place on the cake board and brush with apricot jam. Cover with a thin layer of marzipan and then white sugarpaste icing. Leave to dry overnight.

3 Using the template, carefully mark the position of the teddy on to the cake.

4 Put the coconut into a bowl and mix in a drop of blue colouring to colour it pale blue. Spread a thin layer of royal icing on to the cake within the outline of the teddy. Before the icing dries, sprinkle on some pale blue coconut and press it down lightly.

5 Roll out the sugarpaste trimmings and cut out a nose, ears and paws. Stick in place with a little royal icing. Tint some royal icing black and pipe on the eyes, nose and mouth. Use the red bow as a tie and attach in place with royal icing. Pipe a white royal icing border around the base of the cake, tie the ribbon around the cake and position the candles on top.

Energy 7900kcal/33215kJ; Fat 331.4g, Saturated fat 90.4g; Carbohydrate 1226.6g; Fibre 19.2g

Iced Fancies

These cakes are ideal for a children's tea-party. Ready-made cake decorating products may be used instead, if you like.

Makes 16
115g/4oz/½ cup butter, at room temperature
225g/8oz/generous 1 cup caster (superfine) sugar
2 eggs, at room temperature
175g/6oz/1½ cups plain (all-purpose) flour
1.5ml/¼ tsp salt
7.5ml/1½ tsp baking powder
120ml/4fl oz/½ cup milk
5ml/1 tsp vanilla extract

For the icing
2 large egg whites
400g/14oz/3½ cups sifted icing (confectioners') sugar
1–2 drops glycerine
juice of 1 lemon
food colourings of your choice
coloured vermicelli, and crystallized lemon and orange slices, to decorate

1 Preheat the oven to 190°C/375°F/Gas 5. Line a 16-cup bun tray with paper cases.

2 Cream the butter and sugar until light and fluffy. Add the eggs, one at a time, beating well after each addition.

3 Sift over and stir in the flour, salt and baking powder, alternating with the milk. Add the vanilla extract.

4 Half-fill the cups and bake for about 20 minutes, or until the tops spring back when touched. Stand in the tray to cool for 5 minutes, then unmould on to a wire rack.

5 To make the icing, beat the egg whites until stiff. Gradually add the sugar, glycerine and lemon juice, and beat for 1 minute.

6 Tint the icing with the different food colourings, and use to ice the tops of the cakes.

7 Decorate the cakes with coloured vermicelli and crystallized lemon and orange slices. You can also make freehand decorations such as animal faces using a paper piping (icing) bag.

Energy 259kcal/1094kJ; Fat 6.9g, Saturated fat 4g; Carbohydrate 49.7g; Fibre 0.3g

Fairy Castle Cake

If the icing on this cake dries too quickly, dip a metal spatula into hot water to help smooth the surface.

Makes one cake
20cm/8in round sponge cake
115g/4oz/½ cup butter icing
45ml/3 tbsp apricot jam, warmed and sieved
675g/1½lb/4½ cups marzipan
8 mini Swiss rolls (jelly rolls)
675g/1½lb/4½ cups royal icing
red, blue and green food colouring
jelly diamonds
4 ice cream cones
2 ice cream wafers
50g/2oz/⅔ cup desiccated (dry unsweetened shredded) coconut
8 marshmallows

Materials/equipment
30cm/12in square cake board
wooden cocktail stick (toothpick)

1 Split the cake and fill with butter icing, place in the centre of the board and brush with apricot jam. Cover with a layer of marzipan.

2 Cover each of the Swiss rolls (jelly rolls) with marzipan. Stick four of them around the cake and cut the other four in half.

3 Tint two-thirds of the royal icing pale pink and cover the cake. Ice the extra pieces of Swiss roll and stick them around the top of the cake.

4 Use a cocktail stick to score the walls with a brick pattern. Make windows on the corner towers from jelly diamonds. Cut the ice cream cones to make the tower spires and stick them in place. Leave to dry overnight.

5 Tint half the remaining royal icing pale blue and cover the cones. Use a fork to pattern the icing. Shape the wafers for the gates, stick to the cake and cover with blue icing. Use the back of a knife to mark planks.

6 Tint the coconut with a few drops of green colouring. Spread the board with the remaining royal icing and sprinkle over the coconut. Stick on the marshmallows with a little royal icing to make the small turrets.

Energy 9249kcal/38959kJ; Fat 342.6g, Saturated fat 82.4g; Carbohydrate 1545.3g; Fibre 19.1g

Sailing Boat

For chocoholics, make this cake using chocolate sponge.

Makes one cake
20cm/8in square sponge cake
225g/8oz/1 cup butter icing
15ml/1 tbsp unsweetened
  cocoa powder
4 large flaked chocolate bars
blue and red powder tints
115g/4oz/³⁄₄ cup royal icing
blue food colouring

Materials/equipment
25cm/10in square cake board
rice paper
paintbrush
plastic drinking straw
wooden cocktail stick (toothpick)
2 small cake ornaments

1 Split the cake and fill with half of the butter icing. Cut 7cm/2¾in from one side of the cake. Shape the larger piece to resemble the hull of a boat. Place diagonally across the cake board.

2 Mix the cocoa powder into the remaining butter icing and spread evenly over the top and sides of the boat.

3 Make the rudder and tiller from short lengths of flaked chocolate bars and place them at the stern of the boat. Split the rest of the flaked chocolate bars lengthways and press on to the sides of the boat, horizontally, to resemble planks of wood. Sprinkle the crumbs over the top.

4 Cut two rice paper rectangles, one 14 x 16cm/5¾ x 6½in and the other 15 x 7.5cm/6 x 3in. Cut the bigger one in a gentle curve to make the large sail and the smaller one into a triangle. Brush a circle of blue powder tint on to the large sail.

5 Wet the edges of the sails and stick on to the straw. Make a hole for the straw 7.5cm/3in from the bow of the boat and push into the cake.

6 Cut a rice paper flag and brush with red powder tint. Stick the flag on to a cocktail stick and insert into the top of the straw. Tint the royal icing blue and spread on the board in waves. Place the small ornaments on the boat.

Energy 5147kcal/21498kJ; Fat 310.1g, Saturated fat 104.6g; Carbohydrate 568g; Fibre 9.6g

Spider Cake

A delightfully spooky cake for any occasion, fancy dress or otherwise.

Makes one 900g/2lb cake
900g/2lb dome-shaped lemon
  sponge cake
225g/8oz/³⁄₄ cup lemon-flavour
  glacé icing
black and yellow food colouring

For the spiders
115g/4oz plain chocolate, broken
  into pieces
150ml/¼ pint/²⁄₃ cup double
  (heavy) cream
45ml/3 tbsp ground almonds
unsweetened cocoa powder,
  for dusting
chocolate vermicelli
2–3 liquorice wheels, sweet
  centres removed
15g/½oz/2 tbsp sugarpaste icing

Materials/equipment
small baking parchment piping
  (icing) bag
wooden skewer
20cm/8in cake board

1 Place the cake on baking parchment. Tint 45ml/3 tbsp of the glacé icing black. Tint the rest yellow and pour it over the cake, letting it run down the side.

2 Fill a piping bag with the black icing and, starting at the centre top, drizzle it round the cake in an evenly-spaced spiral. Finish the web by drawing downwards through the icing with a skewer. When set, place on the cake board.

3 To make the spiders, gently melt the chocolate with the cream, stirring frequently. Transfer to a bowl, allow to cool, then beat the mixture for 10 minutes, or until thick and pale. Stir in the ground almonds, then chill until firm enough to handle. Dust your hands with a little cocoa, then make walnut-size balls with the mixture. Roll the balls in chocolate vermicelli.

4 For the legs, cut the liquorice into 4cm/1½in lengths. Make holes in the sides of the spiders and insert the legs. For the spiders' eyes, tint a piece of sugarpaste icing black and form into tiny balls. Make larger balls with white icing. Stick on using water. Arrange the spiders on and around the cake.

Energy 6266kcal/26208kJ; Fat 358.4g, Saturated fat 119.8g; Carbohydrate 734.2g; Fibre 14.5g

Toy Telephone Cake

Very small children love to chat on the phone so this cake would be sure to appeal. The child's name could be piped in a contrasting colour of icing, if you wish.

Makes one cake

15cm/6in square sponge cake
50g/2oz/¼ cup butter icing
30ml/2 tbsp apricot jam, warmed and sieve
275g/10oz marzipan
350g/12oz/2¼ cups sugarpaste icing
yellow, blue, red and black food colouring
liquorice strips
115g/4oz/¾ cup royal icing

Materials/equipment

20cm/8in square cake board
piping nozzle
small baking parchment piping (icing) bag
very fine writing nozzle

1 Split the cake and fill with butter icing. Trim to the shape of a telephone. Round off the edges and cut a shallow groove where the receiver rests on the telephone. Place the cake on the cake board and brush with apricot jam.

2 Cover the cake with marzipan and then cover with the sugarpaste icing. Tint half the remaining sugarpaste icing yellow, a small piece blue and the rest of the icing red.

3 To make the dial, cut out an 8cm/3½in diameter circle in yellow and a 4cm/1½in diameter circle in blue. Stamp out 12 red discs for the numbers with the end of a piping nozzle and cut out a red receiver. Position on the cake with water.

4 Twist the liquorice around to form a curly cord and use royal icing to stick one end to the telephone and the other end to the receiver. Tint the royal icing black and pipe the numbers on the discs and the child's name on the telephone.

> ### Variation
> If you like, you could cut the cake into two rectangles and make a modern push-button phone with its receiver lying beside it.

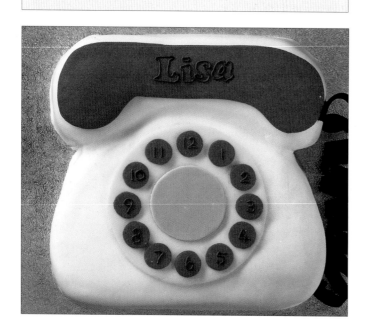

Energy 6250kcal/26250kJ; Fat 277.2g, Saturated fat 64.9g; Carbohydrate 929g; Fibre 12.4g

Bumble Bee Cake

The edible sugar flowers that are used to decorate this cake were bought ready-made but you can make your own if you like.

Makes one cake

20cm/8in round sponge cake
115g/4oz/½ cup butter icing
45ml/3 tbsp apricot jam, warmed and sieved
350g/12oz marzipan
500g/1¼lb/3¾ cups sugarpaste icing
yellow, black, blue and red food colouring
115g/4oz/¾ cup royal icing
50g/2oz/⅔ cup desiccated (dry unsweetened shredded) coconut
6 sugarpaste daisies

Materials/equipment

25cm/10in square cake board
1 paper doily
adhesive tape
1 pipe cleaner

1 Split the cake and fill with butter icing. Cut in half to make semicircles, sandwich the halves together and stand upright on the cake board. Trim the ends to shape the head and tail.

2 Brush with apricot jam and cover with a layer of marzipan. Tint 350g/12oz/2¼ cups of the sugarpaste icing yellow and use to cover the cake.

3 Tint 115g/4oz/¾ cup of the sugarpaste icing black. Roll out and cut three stripes, each 2.5 x 25cm/1 x 10in. Space evenly on the cake and stick on with water.

4 Use the remaining icing to make the eyes and mouth, tinting the icing blue for the pupils and pink for the mouth. Stick on with water.

5 Tint the coconut with a drop of yellow colouring. Cover the cake board with royal icing then sprinkle with coconut. Place the daisies on the board.

6 To make the wings, cut the doily in half, wrap each half into a cone shape and stick together with adhesive tape. Cut the pipe cleaner in half and stick the pieces into the cake, just behind the head. Place the wings over the pipe cleaners.

Energy 7859kcal/33037kJ; Fat 334.1g, Saturated fat 102.8g; Carbohydrate 1212.8g; Fibre 20.7g

Fire Engine Cake

This bright and jolly fire engine is simplicity itself as the decorations are mainly bought sweets and novelties.

Makes one 20 x 10cm/ 8 x 4in cake
20cm/8in square sponge cake
115g/4oz/½ cup butter icing
45ml/3 tbsp apricot jam, warmed and sieved
350g/12oz marzipan
450g/1lb/3 cups sugarpaste icing
red, black and green food colouring
liquorice strips
115g/4oz/4 tbsp royal icing
sweets (candies)
50g/2oz/1⅔ cup desiccated (dry unsweetened shredded) coconut

Materials/equipment
25cm/10in round cake board
small baking parchment piping (icing) bag
fine plain nozzle
2 silver bells
candles and holders

1 Split the cake and fill with the butter icing. Cut in half and sandwich one half on top of the other. Place on the cake board and brush with apricot jam.

2 Trim a thin wedge off the front edge to make a sloping windscreen. Cover with marzipan. Tint 350g/12oz/2¼ cups of the sugarpaste icing red and use to cover the cake.

3 For the ladder, cut the liquorice into two strips and some short pieces for the rungs. Tint half the royal icing black and use some to stick the ladder to the top of the cake.

4 Roll out the remaining sugarpaste icing, cut out windows and stick them on to the cake with a little water.

5 Pipe around the windows in black royal icing using the fine plain nozzle. Stick sweets in place for headlights, lamps and wheels and stick the silver bells on the roof.

6 Tint the coconut green, spread a little royal icing over the cake board and sprinkle with the coconut so that it resembles grass. Stick sweets to the board with royal icing and press the candles into the sweets.

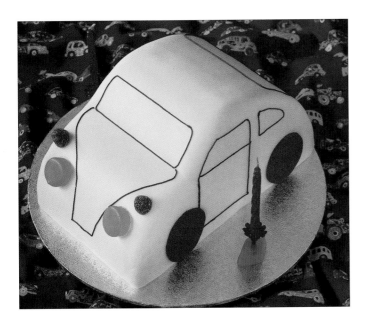

Toy Car Cake

You can add a personalized number plate with the child's name and age to the back of this bright yellow car, if you like.

Makes one car-shaped cake
20cm/8in round sponge cake
115g/4oz/½ cup butter icing
45ml/3 tbsp apricot jam, warmed and sieved
450g/1lb marzipan
500g/1¼lb/3¾ cups sugarpaste icing
yellow, red and black food colouring
30ml/2 tbsp royal icing
red and green sweets (candies)

Materials/equipment
25cm/10in round cake board
wooden cocktail stick (toothpick)
cutters, 4cm/1½in and 2.5cm/1in
small baking parchment piping (icing) bag
very fine writing nozzle
candles and holders

1 Split the cake and fill with the butter icing. Cut in half and sandwich the halves together. Stand upright and slice off pieces to create the windscreen and bonnet. Place on the cake board and brush with apricot jam.

2 Cut a strip of marzipan to cover the top of the cake to level the joins. Then cover the cake all over with marzipan.

3 Tint 450g/1lb/3 cups of the sugarpaste icing yellow and use to cover the cake. Leave to dry overnight.

4 Mark the outlines of the doors and windows on to the car with a cocktail stick.

5 Tint the remaining sugarpaste icing red. Cut out four wheels with the larger cutter. Stick in place with water. Mark the hubs in the centre of each wheel with the smaller cutter.

6 Tint the royal icing black and pipe over the outline marks of the doors and windows.

7 Stick on sweets for headlights with royal icing. Press the candles into sweets and stick to the board with royal icing.

Energy 7749kcal/32592kJ; Fat 315.8g, Saturated fat 77.1g; Carbohydrate 1225g; Fibre 15.8g

Energy 7662kcal/32196kJ; Fat 334.1g, Saturated fat 102.8g; Carbohydrate 1160.6g; Fibre 20.7g

Sandcastle Cake

Crushed digestive biscuits (graham crackers) make realistic-looking sand when used to cover this cake.

Makes one 15cm/6in round cake

2 x 15cm/6in round
   sponge cakes
115g/4oz/½ cup butter icing
45ml/3 tbsp apricot jam, warmed
   and sieved

115g/4oz digestive biscuits
   (graham crackers)
115g/4oz/¾ cup royal icing
blue food colouring
shrimp-shaped
   sweets (candies)

Materials/equipment

25cm/10in square cake board
rice paper
plastic drinking straw
4 candles and holders

1 Split both of the cakes, then sandwich all the layers together with the butter icing. Place in the centre of the cake board.

2 Cut 3cm/1¼in off the top just above the filling and set aside. Shape the rest of the cake with slightly sloping sides.

3 Cut four 3cm/1¼in cubes from the reserved piece of cake. Stick on the cubes for the turrets and brush with apricot jam.

4 Crush the digestive biscuits and press through a sieve to make the "sand". Press some crumbs on to the cake, using a metal spatula to get a smooth finish.

5 Colour some royal icing blue and spread on the board around the sandcastle to make a moat.

6 Spread a little royal icing on to the board around the outside edge of the moat and sprinkle on some crumbs.

7 To make the flag, cut a small rectangle of rice paper and stick on to half a straw with water. Push the end of the straw into the cake.

8 Stick candles into each turret and arrange the shrimp-shaped sweets on the board.

Energy 5154kcal/21569kJ; Fat 282g, Saturated fat 82.8g; Carbohydrate 633.9g; Fibre 9.7g

Clown Face Cake

Children will love this clown whose bright, frilly collar is surprisingly simple to make.

edible silver balls
red, green, blue and black
   food colouring

Makes one 20cm/8in cake

20cm/8in round sponge cake
115g/4oz/½ cup butter icing
45ml/3 tbsp apricot jam, warmed
   and sieved
450g/1lb marzipan
450g/1lb/3 cups sugarpaste icing
115g/4oz/¾ cup royal icing

Materials/equipment

25cm/10in round cake board
small baking parchment piping
   (icing) bag
medium star nozzle
wooden cocktail stick (toothpick)
cotton wool (cotton balls)
candles and holders

1 Split the cake and fill with butter icing. Place on the cake board and brush with apricot jam. Cover with a thin layer of marzipan then with white sugarpaste icing. Mark the position of the features. Using the star nozzle, pipe stars around the base of the cake with some royal icing, placing silver balls on some of the stars as you work, and leave to dry overnight.

2 Make a paper template for the face and features. Tint half the remaining sugarpaste icing pink and cut out the face base. Tint and cut out all the features, rolling a thin sausage to make the mouth. Cut thin strands for the hair. Stick all the features and hair in place with a little water.

3 Tint the remaining sugarpaste icing green. Cut three strips 4cm/1½in wide. Give each a scalloped edge and stretch by rolling a cocktail stick along it to make the frill. Stick the frills on with water and arrange, holding them in place with cotton wool until dry. Put the candles at the top of the head.

> **Cook's Tip**
> *For colouring sugarpaste always use paste colours, as liquid colours will make the sugarpaste too wet; this is especially important when you are making a strong or dark colour.*

Energy 7422kcal/31187kJ; Fat 323.2g, Saturated fat 81.8g; Carbohydrate 1120.6g; Fibre 15.8g

Pinball Machine

Make this brightly coloured cake for the pinball wizard in your life.

Serves 8–10

25cm/10in square sponge cake
225g/8oz/1½ cups butter icing
45ml/3 tbsp apricot jam, warmed and sieved
450g/1lb marzipan
115g/4oz/¾ cup royal icing
450g/1lb/3 cups sugarpaste icing

yellow, blue, green and red food colouring
sweets (candies)
2 ice cream fan wafers

Materials/equipment

20cm/8in round cake tin (pan)
30cm/12in square cake board
small baking parchment piping (icing) bag
no.1 writing nozzle

1 Split the sponge cake and fill with butter icing. Cut off a 5cm/2in strip from one side and reserve. Cut a thin wedge off the top of the cake, diagonally along its length, to end just above the halfway mark. This will give a sloping table.

2 Using the round cake tin (pan) as a guide, cut the reserved strip of cake to make a rounded back for the pinball table. Brush the back and table with apricot jam, then cover separately with marzipan and place on the board. Stick them together with royal icing. Leave to dry overnight.

3 Cover with a layer of sugarpaste icing and leave to dry. Use a template to mark out the pinball design on the top of the cake. Colour the remaining sugarpaste icing yellow, blue, green and pink. Roll out the colours and cut to fit the design. Stick on the pieces with water and smooth the joins carefully.

4 Using royal icing, stick sweets on the cake as buffers, flippers, lights and knobs. Roll some blue sugarpaste icing into a long sausage and use to add an edge to the pinball table and divider.

5 Cut zigzags for the sides and a screen for the back. Stick on with water. Stick the ice cream fans at the back of the screen. Load the pinball sweets. Add the child's name on the screen with iced letters or piping.

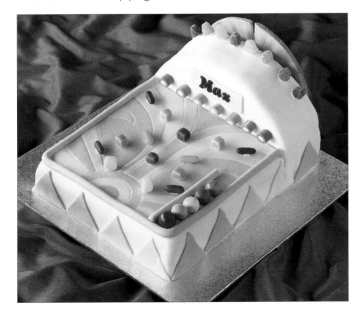

Pirate's Hat

If you prefer, buy ready-made black sugarpaste icing for the hat rather than tinting it yourself.

Serves 8–10

25cm/10in round sponge cake
225g/8oz/1 cup butter icing
45ml/3 tbsp apricot jam, warmed and sieved
450g/1lb marzipan

500g/1¼lb/3¾ cups sugarpaste icing
black and gold food colouring
chocolate money
jewel sweets (candies)

Materials/equipment

30cm/12in square cake board
fine paintbrush

1 Split the cake and fill with butter icing. Cut in half and sandwich the halves together. Stand upright diagonally across the cake board and cut shallow dips from each end to create the brim of the hat. Brush with apricot jam.

2 Cut a strip of marzipan to lay over the top of the cake. Then cover the whole of the cake with a layer of marzipan. Tint 450g/1lb/3 cups of the sugarpaste icing black. Use to cover the cake.

3 Roll out the remaining sugarpaste icing and cut some 1cm/½in strips. Stick the strips in place with a little water around the brim of the pirate's hat and mark with the prongs of a fork to make a braid.

4 Make a skull and crossbones template and mark on to the hat. Cut the shapes out of the white sugarpaste icing and stick in place with water. Paint the braid strip gold and arrange the chocolate money and jewel sweets on the board.

Variation
To make a sandy board for your pirate's hat to rest on, simply cover the board with a thin layer of butter icing and sprinkle finely crushed cookies over.

Energy 792kcal/3320kJ; Fat 40.5g, Saturated fat 15.7g; Carbohydrate 106.9g; Fibre 1.4g

Energy 699kcal/2938kJ; Fat 30.3g, Saturated fat 9.2g; Carbohydrate 106.8g; Fibre 1.4g

Noah's Ark Cake

This charming cake is decorated with small animals, about 4cm/1½in high, available from cake decorating stores.

Makes one 20 x 13cm/ 8 x 5in cake

20cm/8in square sponge cake
115g/4oz/½ cup butter icing
45ml/3 tbsp apricot jam, warmed and sieved

450g/1lb marzipan
450g/1lb/3 cups sugarpaste icing
brown, yellow and blue food colouring
115g/4oz/¾ cup royal icing
chocolate mint stick

Materials/equipment

25cm/10in square cake board
skewer
rice paper
small animal cake ornaments

1 Split the cake and fill with butter icing. Cut off and set aside a 7.5cm/3in strip. Shape the remaining piece of cake to form the hull of the boat. Place diagonally on the cake board.

2 Use the set-aside piece of cake to cut a rectangle 10 x 6cm/ 4 x 2½in for the cabin and a triangular piece for the roof. Sandwich the roof and the cabin with butter icing or apricot jam.

3 Cover the three pieces with a layer of marzipan. Tint the sugarpaste icing brown and use most of it to cover the hull and cabin.

4 Use the remaining brown icing to make a long sausage. Stick around the edge of the hull with water. Mark planks with the back of a knife. Leave to dry overnight.

5 Tint one-third of the royal icing yellow and spread it over the cabin roof with a metal spatula. Roughen it with a skewer to create a thatch effect.

6 Tint the remaining royal icing blue and spread over the cake board, making rough waves. Cut a small triangle out of rice paper to make a flag. Stick the flag on to the chocolate mint stick and press on the back of the boat. Stick the small animals on to the boat with a dab of icing.

Balloons Cake

This is a simple yet effective cake design that can be adapted to suit any age.

Makes one 20cm/8in round cake

20cm/8in round cake
115g/4oz/½ cup butter icing
45ml/3 tbsp apricot jam, warmed and sieved
450g/1lb marzipan
450g/1lb/3 cups sugarpaste icing

red, blue, green and yellow food colouring
115g/4oz/¾ cup royal icing

Materials/equipment

25cm/10in round cake board
2 small baking parchment piping (icing) bags
fine plain and medium star nozzles
1.5m/1½yd blue ribbon
candles and holders

1 Split the cake and fill with butter icing. Place on the cake board and brush with apricot jam. Cover with a layer of marzipan then sugarpaste icing.

2 Divide the remaining sugarpaste icing into three pieces and tint pink, blue and green. Make a balloon template, roll out the coloured sugarpaste and cut out one balloon from each colour. Stick on to the cake with water and rub the edges gently to round them off.

3 Tint the royal icing yellow. With a plain nozzle, pipe on the balloon strings and then pipe a number on to each balloon. Using the star nozzle, pipe a border around the base of the cake.

4 Tie the ribbon around the cake and place the candles in their holders on top.

Cook's Tip

If you are not a fan of marzipan, it is not necessary to cover any sponge cake with marzipan that you will be covering with sugarpaste. Simply spread a thin layer of butter icing over the cake first to stick the sugarpaste.

Energy 6888kcal/28960kJ; Fat 288.6g, Saturated fat 71.3g; Carbohydrate 1068.1g; Fibre 14.9g

Energy 6888kcal/28960kJ; Fat 288.6g, Saturated fat 71.3g; Carbohydrate 1068.1g; Fibre 14.9g

Horse Stencil Cake

Make this cake for a horse lover. You can find stencils at art stores or sugarcraft suppliers. Use a fairly dry brush when painting the design on this cake and allow each colour to dry before adding the next.

Makes one 20cm/8in round cake

20cm/8in round sponge cake
115g/4oz/½ cup butter icing
45ml/3 tbsp apricot jam, warmed and sieved

450g/1lb marzipan
450g/1lb/3 cups sugarpaste icing
yellow, brown, black, red, orange and blue food colouring

Materials/equipment
25cm/10in round cake board
fine paintbrush
spoon with decorative handle
horse and letter stencils
1.5m/1½yd blue ribbon
candles and holders

1 Split the cake and fill with butter icing. Place on the cake board and brush with apricot jam. Cover with a layer of marzipan.

2 Tint the sugarpaste icing yellow, roll out and use to cover the cake. Roll the trimmings into two thin ropes, long enough to go halfway round the cake. Brush water in a thin band around the base of the cake, lay on the ropes and press together. Pattern the border with the decorative spoon handle. Leave to dry overnight.

3 If you do not have a stencil, make one by tracing a simple design on to a piece of thin card (stock) and cutting out the shape with a craft (utility) knife.

4 Place the horse stencil in the centre of the cake. With a fairly dry brush, gently paint over the parts you want to colour first. Allow these to dry completely before adding another colour, otherwise the colours will run into each other. Clean the stencil between colours.

5 When the horse picture is finished carefully paint on the lettering. Tie the ribbon around the side of the cake and place the candles in their holders on top.

Dolls' House Cake

This is a very straightforward cake to make and is decorated with store-bought flowers, or you can make your own if you like.

Serves 8–10
25cm/10in square sponge cake
225g/8oz/1 cup butter icing
45ml/3 tbsp apricot jam, warmed and sieved
450g/1lb marzipan
450g/1lb/3 cups sugarpaste icing

red, yellow, blue, black, green and gold food colouring
115g/4oz/¾ cup royal icing

Materials/equipment
30cm/12in square cake board
pastry wheel
large and fine paintbrushes
wooden cocktail stick (toothpick)
small baking parchment piping (icing) bags
fine writing nozzle
flower decorations

1 Split the cake and fill with butter icing. Cut triangles off two corners and use the pieces to make a chimney. Place on the cake board and brush with apricot jam. Cover with a layer of marzipan then sugarpaste icing.

2 Mark the roof with a pastry wheel and the chimney with the back of a knife. Paint the chimney red and the roof yellow.

3 Tint 25g/1oz/2 tbsp of sugarpaste icing red and cut out a 7.5 x 12cm/3 x 4½in door. Tint enough sugarpaste icing blue to make a fanlight. Stick to the cake with water.

4 Mark windows, 6cm/2½in square, with a cocktail stick. Paint on curtains with blue food colouring. Tint half the royal icing black and pipe around the windows and the door.

5 Tint the remaining royal icing green. Pipe the flower stems and leaves under the windows with the fine writing nozzle and the climber up on to the roof. Stick the flowers in place with a little icing and pipe green flower centres.

6 Pipe the house number or child's age on the door and add a knocker and handle. Leave to dry for 1 hour, then paint with gold food colouring.

Energy 6691kcal/28120kJ; Fat 288.6g, Saturated fat 71.3g; Carbohydrate 1015.9g; Fibre 14.9g

Energy 832kcal/3496kJ; Fat 35.7g, Saturated fat 10.3g; Carbohydrate 127.8g; Fibre 1.6g

Treasure Chest Cake

Allow yourself a few days before the party to make this cake as the lock and handles need to dry for 48 hours.

Makes one 20 x 10cm/ 8 x 4in cake

20cm/8in square sponge cake
115g/4oz/½ cup butter icing
45ml/3 tbsp apricot jam, warmed and sieved
350g/12oz marzipan
400g/14oz/generous 2½ cups sugarpaste icing

brown and green food colouring
50g/2oz/⅔ cup desiccated (dry unsweetened shredded) coconut
115g/4oz/¾ cup royal icing
edible gold dusting powder
edible silver balls
chocolate money

Materials/equipment
30cm/12in round cake board
fine paintbrush

1 Split the cake and fill with butter icing. Cut the cake in half and sandwich the halves on top of each other with butter icing. Place on the cake board.

2 Shape the top of the cake into a rounded lid (you could make a paper template to use on the ends if you like) and brush with apricot jam. Cover with a layer of marzipan. Tint 350g/12oz/2¼ cups of the sugarpaste icing brown and use to cover the cake.

3 Use the brown sugarpaste trimmings to make strips. Stick on to the chest with water. Mark the lid with a sharp knife. Tint the coconut with a few drops of green colouring. Spread a little royal icing over the cake board and press the green coconut lightly into it to make the grass.

4 From the remaining sugarpaste icing, cut out the padlock and two handles. Cut a keyhole shape from the padlock and shape the handles over a small box. Leave to dry for 48 hours. Stick the padlock and handles in place with royal icing and paint them with the gold dusting powder. Stick silver balls on to look like nails. Arrange the chocolate money around the chest on the board.

Energy 6600kcal/27758kJ; Fat 269.6g, Saturated fat 69.7g; Carbohydrate 1045.1g; Fibre 12g.

Lion Cake

For an animal lover or a celebration cake for a Leo horoscope sign, this cake is ideal. The shaggy mane is simply made with grated marzipan.

Makes one 28 x 23cm/ 11 x 9in oval cake

25 x 30cm/10 x 12in sponge cake
350g/12oz/1½ cups orange-
flavour butter icing
orange and red food colouring
675g/1½lb yellow marzipan
50g/2oz/generous 4 tbsp sugarpaste icing
red and orange liquorice bootlaces
long and round marshmallows

Materials/equipment
30cm/12in square cake board
small heart-shaped cutter

1 With the flat side of the cake uppermost, cut it to make an oval shape with an uneven scallop design around the edge. Turn the cake over and trim the top level.

2 Place the cake on the cake board. Tint the butter icing orange and use it to cover the cake.

3 Roll 115g/4oz/¾ cup of marzipan to a 15cm/6in square. Place in the centre of the cake for the lion's face.

4 Grate the remaining marzipan and use to cover the sides and the top of the cake up to the face panel.

5 Tint the sugarpaste icing red. Use the heart-shaped cutter to stamp out the lion's nose and position on the cake with water.

6 Roll the remaining red icing into two thin, short strands to make the lion's mouth, and stick on with water.

7 Cut the liquorice into graduated lengths, and place on the cake for the whiskers.

8 Use two flattened round marshmallows for the eyes and two snipped long ones for the eyebrows and place in position on the cake.

Energy 8108kcal/33970kJ; Fat 426.6g, Saturated fat 131.5g; Carbohydrate 1043.6g; Fibre 20g

Train Cake

This cake is made in a train-shaped tin, so all you need to do is decorate it.

Makes one train-shaped cake

train-shaped sponge cake, about
   35cm/14in long
675g/1½lb/3 cups butter icing
yellow food colouring
red liquorice bootlaces

90–120ml/6–8 tbsp
   coloured vermicelli
4 liquorice wheels

Materials/equipment

25 x 38cm/10 x 15in cake board
2 fabric piping bags
fine round and small star nozzles
pink and white cotton wool
   (cotton balls)

1 Slice off the top surface of the cake to make it flat. Place diagonally on the cake board.

2 Tint the butter icing yellow. Use half of it to cover the cake.

3 Using a round piping nozzle and a quarter of the remaining butter icing, pipe a straight double border around the top edge of the cake.

4 Place the red liquorice bootlaces on the piped border. Snip the bootlaces around the curves on the train.

5 Using a small star nozzle and the remaining butter icing, pipe small stars over the top of the cake. Add extra liquorice and piping, if you like. Use a metal spatula to press on the coloured vermicelli all around the sides of the cake.

6 Pull a couple of balls of cotton wool apart for the steam and stick on to the cake board with butter icing. Press the liquorice wheels in place for the wheels.

> **Cook's Tip**
> *You can buy novelty cake tins (pans) in all kinds of shapes or hire them from specialist cake suppliers if you are not confident that you could shape your cake well.*

Number 7 Cake

Any combination of colours will work well for this cake with its marbled effect.

Makes one 30cm/12in long cake

23 x 30cm/9 x 12in sponge cake
350g/12oz/1½ cups orange-
   flavour butter icing
60ml/4 tbsp apricot jam, warmed
   and sieved

675g/1½lb/4½ cups
   sugarpaste icing
blue and green
   food colouring
rice paper sweets

Materials/equipment

25 x 33cm/10 x 13in cake board
small "7" cutter

1 Place the cake flat side up and cut out the number seven. Slice the cake horizontally, sandwich together with the butter icing and place on the board.

2 Brush the cake evenly with apricot jam. Divide the sugarpaste icing into three and tint one of the pieces blue and another green. Set aside 50g/2oz/scant ½ cup from each of the coloured icings. Knead together the large pieces of blue and green icing with the third piece of white icing to marble. Use to cover the cake.

3 Immediately after covering, use the "7" cutter to remove several sugarpaste shapes in a random pattern from the covered cake.

4 Roll out the reserved blue and green sugarpaste icing and stamp out shapes with the same cutter. Use these to fill the stamped-out shapes from the cake. Decorate the board with some rice paper sweets.

> **Cook's Tip**
> *You could make any number out of sponge cake using round and/or rectangular cakes (or you could hire a purpose-made tin (pan) instead). Use two cakes for numbers in their teens and over.*

Musical Cake

Creating a sheet of music requires delicate piping work, so it is best to practise first.

**Makes one 20 x 25cm/
8 x 10in cake**
25cm/10in square sponge cake
225g/8oz/1 cup butter icing
45ml/3 tbsp apricot jam, warmed
  and sieved
450g/1lb marzipan
450g/1lb/3 cups sugarpaste icing

115g/4oz/³⁄₄ cup royal icing
black food colouring

Materials/equipment
25 x 30cm/10 x 12in cake board
wooden cocktail stick (toothpick)
2 small baking parchment piping
  (icing) bags
very fine writing and fine
  shell nozzles
1.5m/1¹⁄₂yd red ribbon

1 Split the cake and fill with a little butter icing. Cut a 5cm/2in strip off one side of the cake. Place the cake on the cake board and brush with apricot jam. Cover with a layer of marzipan then sugarpaste icing. Leave to dry overnight.

2 Make a template for the sheet of music and the child's name. Lay the template on the cake and trace over the music and name with a cocktail stick. Using white royal icing and a very fine writing nozzle, begin by piping the lines and bars. Leave to dry.

3 Tint the remaining icing black and pipe the clefs, name and notes. With the shell nozzle, pipe a royal icing border around the base of the cake. Finally, tie a ribbon around the side.

Cook's Tip
Find a sheet of simple music to copy for the cake – a beginner's piano book would be ideal. Practise writing the treble clef on paper first, and always start at the centre of the symbol: make a dot and then curl round to the right; curl to the left and then up and out to the right to make the loop at the top; finish with the downward line that ends with a curl to the left at the base of the symbol.

Energy 7924kcal/33281kJ; Fat 356.9g, Saturated fat 103.1g; Carbohydrate 1173.1g; Fibre 15.8g

Magic Rabbit Cake

Delight a child with this cute rabbit bursting out of a hat.

**Makes one 15cm/6in tall
round cake**
2 x 15cm/6in round cakes
225g/8oz/1 cup butter icing
115g/4oz/³⁄₄ cup royal icing
45ml/3 tbsp apricot jam, warmed
  and sieved
675g/1¹⁄₂lb marzipan

675g/1¹⁄₂lb/4¹⁄₂ cups sugarpaste
  icing
black and pink food colouring
edible silver balls

Materials/equipment
25cm/10in square cake board
2 small baking parchment piping
  (icing) bags
medium star nozzle
1.5m/1¹⁄₂yd pink ribbon

1 Split the cakes and fill with butter icing, then sandwich them one on top of the other. Stick on the centre of the cake board with a little royal icing. Brush with apricot jam. Use 450g/1lb/3 cups of the marzipan to cover the cake.

2 Tint the sugarpaste icing grey. Use about two-thirds of it to cover the cake. For the hat's brim roll out the remaining grey sugarpaste to a 20cm/8in round. Cut a 15cm/6in circle from its centre. Lower the brim over the cake. Shape the brim sides over wooden spoon handles until dry.

3 Cut a cross in the 15cm/6in grey circle and place on the hat. Curl the triangles over a wooden spoon handle to shape. Smooth the join at the top and sides of the hat using the warmth of your hand

4 Tint the remaining marzipan pink and make the rabbit's head, about 5cm/2in wide with a pointed face. Mark the position of the eyes, nose and mouth. Leave to dry overnight.

5 Stick the rabbit in the centre of the hat with a little royal icing. Pipe a border of royal icing around the top and base of the hat and decorate with silver balls while still wet. Tint the remaining royal icing black and pipe the rabbit's eyes and mouth. Tie the ribbon around the hat.

Energy 10054kcal/42289kJ; Fat 412.7g, Saturated fat 111.2g; Carbohydrate 1586.6g; Fibre 20.9g

Nurse's Kit Cake

The box is easy to make and is simply filled with toys from a nurse's or doctor's set. It's sure to delight any budding medical professionals.

Makes one 20 x 17cm/ 8 x 6½in cake

35 x 20cm/14 x 8in chocolate sponge cake

120ml/4fl oz/½ cup apricot jam, warmed and sieved
675g/1½lb/4½ cups sugarpaste icing
red food colouring

Materials/equipment

25cm/10in square cake board
selection of toy medical equipment

1 Place the cake dome-side down and cut in half widthways.

2 To make the base of the nurse's box, turn one cake half, dome-side up, and hollow out the centre to a depth of 1cm/½in, leaving a 1cm/½in border on the three uncut edges. Brush the tops and sides of both cake halves with jam.

3 Tint 150g/5oz/scant 1 cup sugarpaste icing deep pink. Use a little to make a small handle for the box. Wrap in clear film (plastic wrap) and set aside. Cover the cake board with the remainder of the pink icing. Tint 25g/1oz/2 tbsp of the sugarpaste icing red. Cover with clear film and set aside.

4 Tint the remaining icing light pink and divide into two portions, one slightly bigger than the other. Roll out the bigger portion and use to cover the base of the box, easing it into the hollow and along the edges. Trim, then position the base on the cake board.

5 Roll out the other portion and use to cover the lid of the box. Trim, then place on top of the base at a slight angle.

6 Stick the handle to the base of the box using water. Cut a small cross out of red icing and stick it on the lid. Place a few toy items of medical equipment under the lid, protruding slightly. Arrange some more items around the board and cake.

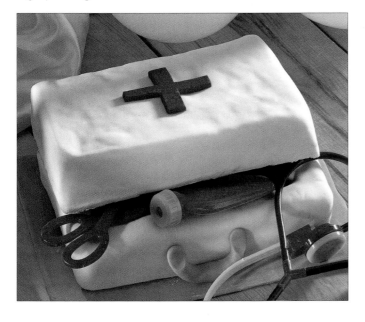

Energy 5993kcal/25233kJ; Fat 237.6g, Saturated fat 0g; Carbohydrate 954.4g; Fibre 0g

Ballerina Cake

Use flower cutters with ejectors to make the tiny flowers for this cake.

Makes one 20cm/8in round cake

20cm/8in round sponge cake
115g/4oz/½ cup butter icing
45ml/3 tbsp apricot jam, warmed and sieved
450g/1lb marzipan
450g/1lb/3 cups sugarpaste icing
pink, yellow, blue and green food colouring
115g/4oz/¾ cup royal icing

Materials/equipment

25cm/10in round cake board
small flower cutter
small circle cutter
wooden cocktail stick (toothpick)
cotton wool (cotton balls)
fine paintbrush
3 small baking parchment piping (icing) bags
fine shell nozzle
1.5m/1½yd pink ribbon

1 Split the cake and fill with butter icing. Place on the board and brush with apricot jam. Cover with marzipan then sugarpaste icing. Leave to dry overnight. Divide the rest of the sugarpaste into three. Tint flesh tone, light pink and dark pink. Stamp out 15 pale pink flowers. Leave to dry.

2 Make a template of the ballerina. Mark her position on the cake. Cut out a flesh-tone body and dark pink bodice. Stick on with water, rounding off the edges.

3 Cut two dark pink underskirts, a pale pink top skirt and a dark pink bodice extension to make the tutu. Stamp out hollow, fluted circles, divide the circles into four and frill the fluted edges with a cocktail stick. Stick the tutu in place, supported with cotton wool. Cut out and stick on pale pink shoes. Leave to dry overnight.

4 Paint the ballerina's face and hair. Position 12 hoop and three headdress flowers. Tint some royal icing green and dark pink to complete the flowers and ballet shoes. Pipe a border around the base with the shell nozzle. Tie the pink ribbon around the outside of the cake.

Energy 6771kcal/28459kJ; Fat 288.6g, Saturated fat 71.3g; Carbohydrate 1037.1g; Fibre 14.9g

Circus Cake

This colourful design is easy to achieve and is sure to delight young children.

Makes one 20cm/8in cake
20cm/8in round sponge cake
115g/4oz/½ cup butter icing
45ml/3 tbsp apricot jam, warmed and sieved
450g/1lb marzipan
450g/1lb/3 cups sugarpaste icing

red and blue food colouring
115g/4oz/¾ cup royal icing
edible silver balls
3 digestive biscuits (graham crackers)

Materials/equipment
25cm/10in round cake board
small baking parchment piping (icing) bag
small star nozzle
5cm/2in plastic circus ornaments

1 Split the cake and fill with butter icing. Place on the cake board and brush with apricot jam. Cover with a layer of marzipan then sugarpaste icing.

2 Tint 115g/4oz/¾ cup sugarpaste icing pink, then roll into a rope and stick around the top edge of the cake with a little water.

3 Tint half the remaining sugarpaste icing red and half blue. Roll out each colour and cut into twelve 2.5cm/1in squares. Stick the squares alternately at an angle around the side of the cake with a little water. Using the star nozzle, pipe stars around the base of the cake with royal icing and stick in the edible silver balls.

4 Crush the digestive biscuits by pressing through a sieve to make the "sand" for the circus ring. Sprinkle the "sand" over the top of the cake and place small circus ornaments on top.

> **Variation**
> *Instead of a circus you could make the cake into an ice rink. Cover the top of the cake with very pale blue marbled sugarpaste (by colouring two or three balls of sugarpaste different shades of pale blue and then rolling them out with the white to get a marbled effect). Then buy some ice skaters to go on the top.*

Monsters on the Moon

A great cake for little monsters! This cake is covered with a sugar frosting and is best eaten on the day of making.

Serves 12–15
1 quantity quick-mix sponge cake
500g/1¼lb/3¾ cups sugarpaste icing
black food colouring
225g/8oz marzipan

edible silver glitter powder (optional)
375g/12oz/1¾ cups caster (superfine) sugar
2 egg whites
60ml/4 tbsp water

Materials/equipment
ovenproof wok
various sizes of plain round and star cutters
30cm/12in round cake board
small monster toys

1 Preheat the oven to 180°C/350°F/Gas 4. Grease the wok and line with baking parchment. Spoon in the cake mixture and smooth the surface.

2 Bake in the centre of the oven for 35–40 minutes. Leave for 5 minutes, then turn out on to a rack and peel off the paper. Leave to cool completely.

3 With the cake dome-side up, use the round cutters to cut out craters. Press in the cutters to about 2.5cm/1in deep, then remove and cut the craters out of the cake with a knife.

4 Use 115g/4oz/¾ cup of the sugarpaste icing to cover the cake, pulling off small pieces and pressing them in uneven strips around the edges of the craters.

5 Tint the remaining sugarpaste icing black. Roll out and cover the board. Stamp out stars and replace with marzipan stars of the same size. Dust with glitter powder, if using, and place on the board.

6 Put the sugar, egg whites and water in a heatproof bowl over a pan of simmering water. Beat until thick and peaky. Spoon the icing over the cake, swirling it into the craters and peaking it unevenly. Sprinkle over the silver glitter powder, if using, then position the monsters on the cake.

Energy 438kcal/1850kJ; Fat 12.8g, Saturated fat 2.5g; Carbohydrate 81.9g; Fibre 0.6g

Energy 6888kcal/28960kJ; Fat 288.6g, Saturated fat 71.3g; Carbohydrate 1068.1g; Fibre 14.9g

Ladybird Cake

Children will love this colourful and appealing ladybird, and it is very simple to make.

Serves 10–12

3-egg quantity quick-mix sponge cake
175g/6oz butter icing
60ml/4 tbsp lemon curd, warmed
icing (confectioners') sugar, for dusting
1kg/2¼lb/6¾ cups sugarpaste icing
red, black and green food colourings
5 marshmallows
50g/2oz marzipan
2 pipe cleaners

1 Preheat the oven to 180°C/350°F/Gas 4. Grease and line the base of a 1.2 litre/2 pint/5 cup ovenproof bowl. Spoon in the cake mixture and smooth the surface. Bake for 55–60 minutes, or until a skewer inserted into the centre comes out clean. Cool.

2 Cut the cake in half crossways and sandwich together with the butter icing. Cut vertically through the cake, about a third of the way in. Brush both pieces with the lemon curd.

3 Colour 450g/1lb/3 cups of the sugarpaste icing red. Dust a work surface with icing sugar and roll out the icing to about 5mm/¼in thick. Use to cover the larger piece of cake to make the body. Using a wooden skewer, make an indentation down the centre for the wings. Colour 350g/12oz of the sugarpaste icing black, roll out three-quarters and use to cover the smaller piece of cake for the head. Place both cakes on a cake board, press together.

4 Roll out 50g/2oz/4 tbsp icing and cut out two 5cm/2in circles for the eyes, stick to the head with water. Roll out the remaining black icing and cut out eight 4cm/1½in circles. Use two of these for the eyes and stick the others on to the body.

5 Colour some icing green and squeeze through a garlic press to make grass. Flatten the marshmallows and stick a marzipan round in the centre of each. Colour the pipe cleaners black and press a ball of black icing on to the end of each for the feelers. Arrange grass on the board, with the decorations.

Frog Prince Cake

Our happy frog will bring a smile to any young child's face – and will probably even get a kiss!

Serves 8–10

20cm/8in round sponge cake
115g/4oz/½ cup butter icing
45ml/3 tbsp apricot jam, warmed and sieved
450g/1lb marzipan
cornflour (cornstarch), for dusting
500g/1¼lb/3¾ cups sugarpaste icing
115g/4oz/¾ cup royal icing
green, red, black and gold food colouring

Materials/equipment

25cm/10in square cake board
glass
fine paintbrush

1 Split the cake and fill with butter icing. Cut in half and sandwich the halves together with apricot jam. Stand upright diagonally across the cake board. Brush the cake with apricot jam and cover with marzipan.

2 Tint 450g/1lb/3 cups of the sugarpaste icing green and cover the cake. Roll the remaining green sugarpaste icing into 1cm/½in diameter sausages. You will need two folded 20cm/8in lengths for the back legs and 14 10cm/4in lengths for the front legs and feet. Stick in place with a little royal icing. Roll balls for the eyes and stick in place.

3 Roll out the reserved sugarpaste icing and cut a 5 x 19cm/2 x 7½in strip. Cut out triangles along one edge to make the crown shape. Wrap around a glass dusted with cornflour and moisten the edges to join. Leave to dry.

4 Cut a 10cm/4in circle for the white shirt. Stick in place and trim the base edge. Cut white circles and stick to the eyes.

5 Tint a little sugarpaste pink, roll into a sausage and stick on for the mouth. Tint the rest black and use for the pupils and the bow tie. Stick in place.

6 Paint the crown with gold food colouring, leave to dry, then stick into position with royal icing.

Energy 681kcal/2862kJ; Fat 28.9g, Saturated fat 7.1g; Carbohydrate 104.7g; Fibre 1.5g

Energy 539kcal/2270kJ; Fat 19.5g, Saturated fat 6.3g; Carbohydrate 92.7g; Fibre 0.5g

Spaceship Cake

The perfect cake for all would-be astronauts.

Serves 10–12

25cm/10in square sponge cake
225g/8oz/1 cup butter icing
60ml/4 tbsp apricot jam, warmed
　and sieved

350g/12oz marzipan
450g/1lb/3 cups sugarpaste icing
blue, red and black food colouring

Materials/equipment
30cm/12in square cake board
silver candles and holders
gold paper stars

1 Split the sponge cake and fill with butter icing. Cut a 10cm/4in wide piece diagonally across the middle of the cake, about 25cm/10in long. Shape the nose end and straighten the other end.

2 From the off-cuts make three 7.5cm/3in triangles for the wings and top of the ship. Cut two smaller triangles for the booster jets.

3 Position the main body, wings and top of the cake diagonally across the cake board. Add extra pieces of cake in front of the triangle on top of the cake to shape it as shown in the picture.

4 Brush the cake and booster jets with apricot jam, then cover with a layer of marzipan and sugarpaste icing.

5 Divide the remaining sugarpaste icing into three. Tint blue, pink and black. Roll out the blue icing and cut it into 1cm/½in strips. Stick around the base of the cake with water and outline the boosters. Cut a 2.5cm/1in strip and stick down the centre of the spaceship.

6 Roll out the pink and black sugarpaste icing separately and cut shapes, numbers and the child's name to finish the design. When complete, position the boosters.

7 Make small cubes with the off-cuts of sugarpaste icing and use to stick the candles to the cake board. Decorate the board with gold stars.

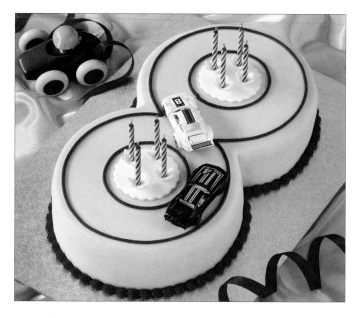

Racing Track Cake

This simple cake will delight eight-year-old racing car enthusiasts.

Serves 10–12

2 x 15cm/6in round sponge cakes
115g/4oz/½ cup butter icing
60ml/4 tbsp apricot jam, warmed
　and sieved
450g/1lb marzipan
500g/1¼lb/3¾ cups
　sugarpaste icing

blue and red food colouring
115g/4oz/¾ cup royal icing

Materials/equipment
25 x 35cm/10 x 14in cake board
5cm/2in fluted cutter
2 small baking parchment piping
　(icing) bags
medium star and medium
　plain nozzles
8 candles and holders
2 small toy racing cars

1 Split the cakes and fill with a little butter icing. Cut off a 1cm/½in piece from the side of each cake and place the cakes on the cake board, cut edges together.

2 Brush the cake with apricot jam and cover with a layer of marzipan. Tint 450g/1lb/3 cups of the sugarpaste icing pale blue and use to cover the cake.

3 Mark a 5cm/2in circle in the centre of each cake. Roll out the remaining white sugarpaste icing, cut out two fluted 5cm/2in circles and stick them in the marked spaces.

4 Tint the royal icing red. Pipe a shell border around the base of the cake using the star nozzle.

5 Pipe a track for the cars using the plain nozzle and stick the candles into the two white circles. Place the cars on the track.

> **Variation**
> *You can adapt this cake by changing the colours or decorating with other shapes, such as colouring the sugarpaste green and adding some toy horses; perhaps add some cut-out flowers to make it look like a meadow.*

Energy 320kcal/1350kJ; Fat 10.6g, Saturated fat 4.6g; Carbohydrate 58.1g; Fibre 0.6g

Energy 624kcal/2624kJ; Fat 26.6g, Saturated fat 6.4g; Carbohydrate 95.7g; Fibre 1.4g

Floating Balloons Cake

Make brightly coloured balloons to float above the cake from eggshells covered in sugarpaste.

Makes one 20cm/8in round cake

20cm/8in round sponge or fruit cake, covered with 800g/1¾lb marzipan if you like
900g/2lb/6 cups sugarpaste icing
red, green and yellow food colouring
3 eggs

2 egg whites
450g/1lb/4 cups icing (confectioners') sugar

Materials/equipment

25cm/10in round cake board
3 bamboo skewers, 25cm/10in, 24cm/9½in and 23cm/9in long
small star cutter
baking parchment piping bags
fine writing nozzle
1m/1yd fine coloured ribbon
candles

1 Using a skewer, pierce the eggs and carefully empty the contents. Wash and dry the shells.

2 Place the cake on the board. Tint 50g/2oz/scant ½ cup of the sugarpaste icing red, 50g/2oz/scant ½ cup green and 115g/4oz/1 cup yellow. Cover the cake with the remaining icing. Use just under half the yellow icing to cover the board.

3 Cover the eggshells carefully with the tinted sugarpaste and insert a bamboo skewer in each. Use the trimmings to stamp out a star shape of each colour. Thread on to the skewers for the balloon knots.

4 Trace 16 balloon shapes on to baking paper. Beat the egg whites with the icing sugar until smooth, and divide between four bowls. Leave one white and tint the others red, green and yellow. With the fine writing nozzle and white icing, trace around the balloon shapes. Thin the tinted icings with water. Fill the balloon shapes using snipped piping bags. Dry overnight.

5 Stick the balloon shapes around the side of the cake with icing. Pipe white balloon strings. Push the large balloons into the centre and decorate with the ribbon. Push the candles into the icing around the edge.

Number 6 Cake

Boys and girls will love this delightful cake.

Serves 10–12

15cm/6in round and 15cm/6in square sponge cakes
115g/4oz/½ cup butter icing
60ml/4 tbsp apricot jam, warmed and sieved
450g/1lb marzipan
500g/1¼lb/3¾ cups sugarpaste icing

yellow and green food colouring
115g/4oz/¾ cup royal icing

Materials/equipment

25 x 35cm/10 x 14in cake board
2 small baking parchment piping (icing) bags
7.5cm/3in fluted cutter
fine plain and medium star nozzles
plastic train set and 6 candles

1 Split the cakes and fill with butter icing. Cut the square cake in half and cut, using the round cake tin as a guide, a rounded end from one rectangle to fit around the round cake. Trim the cakes to the same depth and assemble the number 6 on the cake board. Brush with apricot jam and cover with a thin layer of marzipan.

2 Tint 450g/1lb/3 cups of the sugarpaste icing yellow and the rest green. Cover the cake with the yellow icing.

3 With the cutter, mark a circle in the centre of the round cake. Cut out a green sugarpaste icing circle. Stick in place with water and leave to dry overnight.

4 Mark a track the width of the train on the top of the cake. Tint the royal icing yellow and pipe the track with the plain nozzle. Use the star nozzle to pipe a border around the base and top of the cake. Pipe the name on the green circle and attach the train and candles with royal icing.

> ### Variation
> *You could add a dancer or fairy in the centre and decorate the cake with sugarpaste or commercially made flowers.*

Energy 10835kcal/45729kJ; Fat 335.8g, Saturated fat 59.3g; Carbohydrate 1952.8g; Fibre 22.4g

Energy 667kcal/2801kJ; Fat 28.9g, Saturated fat 6.9g; Carbohydrate 100.9g; Fibre 1.4g

Spider's Web Cake

Make the marzipan spider several days before you need the cake, to give it time to dry.

Makes one 20cm/8in round cake

20cm/8in round deep sponge cake
225g/8oz/1 cup butter icing
45ml/3 tbsp apricot jam, warmed and sieved
30ml/2 tbsp unsweetened cocoa powder
chocolate vermicelli

40g/1½oz marzipan
yellow, red, black and brown food colouring
225g/8oz/1½ cups icing (confectioners') sugar
15–30ml/1–2 tbsp water

Materials/equipment
25cm/10in round cake board
2 small baking parchment piping (icing) bags
wooden cocktail stick (toothpick)
medium star nozzle
candles and holders

1 Split the cake and fill with half the butter icing. Brush the sides with apricot jam, add the cocoa to the remaining butter icing then smooth a little over the sides of the cake. Roll the sides of the cake in chocolate vermicelli. Place on the board.

2 For the spider, tint the marzipan yellow. Roll half of it into two balls of equal size for the head and body. Tint a small piece of marzipan red and make a mouth, and three balls to stick on the spider's body. Tint a tiny piece of marzipan black for the eyes. Roll the rest of the yellow marzipan into eight legs and two smaller feelers. Stick together.

3 Gently heat the icing sugar and water over a pan of hot water. Use two-thirds of the glacé icing to cover the cake top.

4 Tint the remaining glacé icing brown and use it to pipe concentric circles on to the cake. Divide the web into eighths by drawing lines across with a cocktail stick. Leave to set.

5 Put the rest of the chocolate butter icing into a piping bag fitted with a star nozzle and pipe a border around the web. Put candles around the border and the spider in the centre.

Dart Board Cake

This cake is very striking.

Makes one 25cm/10in round cake

25cm/10in round sponge cake
175g/6oz/¾ cup butter icing
5ml/3 tbsp apricot jam, warmed and sieved
450g/1lb marzipan
450g/1lb/3 cups sugarpaste icing
black, red, yellow and silver food colouring

115g/4oz/¾ cup royal icing

Materials/equipment
30cm/12in round cake board
icing smoother
1cm/½in plain circle cutter
small baking parchment piping (icing) bag
fine writing nozzle
3 candles and holders

1 Split the cake and fill with butter icing and put on to the board. Brush with jam and cover with marzipan. Colour some of the sugarpaste icing black, a small piece red and the remainder yellow. Cover the cake with black sugarpaste icing. Cut a 20cm/8in circular template out of baking parchment. Fold it in quarters, then divide each quarter into fifths.

2 Using the template, mark the centre and wedges on the top of the cake with a sharp knife. Cut out ten wedges from the yellow sugarpaste, using the template as a guide. Lay alternate sections on the cake, but do not stick in place yet. Repeat the process with the black sugarpaste. Cut 3mm/⅛in strips off the end of each wedge and swap the colour. Mark a 13cm/5in circle in the centre of the board and cut out 3mm/⅛in strips from each colour to swap with adjoining colours. Stick in place and use an icing smoother to flatten.

3 Use the cutter to remove the centre for the bull's eye. Replace with a circle of red sugarpaste, cut with the same cutter. Surround it with a strip of black sugarpaste. Roll the remaining black sugarpaste into a long sausage to fit round the base of the cake and stick in place with a little water. Mark numbers on the board and pipe on with royal icing using the fine writing nozzle. Leave to dry then paint with silver food colouring. Stick candles in at an angle to resemble darts.

Army Tank Cake

Create an authentic camouflaged tank by combining green and brown sugarpaste icing.

Makes one 25 x 15cm/ 10 x 6in cake

25cm/10in square sponge cake
225g/8oz/1 cup butter icing
45ml/3 tbsp apricot jam, warmed and sieved
450g/1lb marzipan
450g/1lb/3 cups sugarpaste icing brown, green and black food colouring
1 flaked chocolate bar
liquorice strips
60ml/4 tbsp royal icing
round cookies
sweets (candies)

Materials/equipment

25 x 35cm/10 x 14in cake board

1 Split the sponge cake and fill with butter icing. Cut off a 10cm/4in strip from one side of the cake. Use the off-cut to make a 15 x 7.5cm/6 x 3in rectangle, and stick on the top.

2 Shape the sloping top and cut a 2.5cm/1in piece from both ends to form the tracks. Shape the rounded ends for the wheels and tracks. Place on the cake board and brush with apricot jam. Cover with a layer of marzipan.

3 Tint a quarter of the sugarpaste icing brown and the rest green. Roll out the green to a 25cm/10in square. Break small pieces of brown icing and place all over the green. Flatten and roll out together to give a camouflage effect. Turn the icing over and repeat.

4 Continue to roll out until the icing is 3mm/⅛in thick. Lay it over the cake and gently press to fit. Using your hand smooth the sugarpaste around all the curves of the tank. Cut away the excess.

5 From the trimmings cut a piece into a 6cm/2½in disc and stick on the top with a little water. Cut a small hole in the front of the tank for the gun and insert the flaked chocolate. Stick liquorice on for the tracks, using a little black royal icing. Stick on cookies for the wheels and sweets for the lights and portholes.

Camping Tent Cake

Dream of the outdoor life with this fun cake.

Makes one 20 x 10cm/ 8 x 4in cake

20cm/8in square sponge cake
115g/4oz/½ cup butter icing
45ml/3 tbsp apricot jam, warmed and sieved
450g/1lb marzipan
500g/1¼lb/3¾ cups sugarpaste icing
brown, orange, green, red and blue food colouring
50g/2oz/⅓ cup desiccated (dry unsweetened shredded) coconut
115g/4oz/¾ cup royal icing
chocolate mint sticks

Materials/equipment

25cm/10in square cake board
wooden cocktail sticks (toothpicks)
fine paintbrush
4 small baking parchment piping (icing) bags
very fine basketweave and plain nozzles
toy ball

1 Split the cake and fill with butter icing. Cut the cake in half. Cut one half in two diagonally from the top right edge to the bottom left edge to form the roof of the tent. Stick the two wedges, back-to-back, on top of the rectangle with jam. Trim to 10cm/4in high and use the trimmings on the base. Place the cake diagonally on the board and brush with jam.

2 Cover the entire cake with marzipan, reserving some for modelling. Tint 50g/2oz/scant ½ cup of the sugarpaste icing brown and cover one end of the tent. Tint the rest orange and cover the rest of the cake. Cut a semicircle for the tent opening and a central 7.5cm/3in slit. Lay over the brown end. Secure the flaps with royal icing. Put halved cocktail sticks in the corners and ridge.

3 Tint the coconut green. Spread the board with a thin layer of royal icing and sprinkle with the coconut.

4 Tint the reserved marzipan flesh-colour and use to make a model of a child. Paint on a blue T-shirt and leave to dry. Tint some royal icing brown and pipe on the hair with a basketweave nozzle. Tint the icing and pipe on the mouth and eyes. Make a bonfire with broken chocolate mint sticks.

Energy 5636kcal/23658kJ; Fat 262.5g, Saturated fat 93.3g; Carbohydrate 819.4g; Fibre 13.1g

Energy 8226kcal/34566kJ; Fat 360.1g, Saturated fat 103.4g; Carbohydrate 1244.3g; Fibre 16.2g

Chessboard Cake

To make this cake look most effective, ensure that the squares have very sharp and clear edges.

Makes one 25cm/10in square cake

25cm/10in square sponge cake
225g/8oz/1 cup butter icing
60ml/4 tbsp apricot jam, warmed and sieved
800g/1¾lb marzipan

500g/1¼lb/3¾ cups sugarpaste icing
black and red food colouring
edible silver balls
115g/4oz/¾ cup royal icing

Materials/equipment

30cm/12in square cake board
small baking parchment piping (icing) bag
medium star nozzle

1 Split the cake and fill with butter icing. Place on the cake board and brush with jam.

2 Roll out 450g/1lb/3 cups marzipan and use to cover the cake.

3 Once the marzipan has dried, cover with 450g/1lb/3 cups of the sugarpaste icing. Leave to dry overnight.

4 Divide the remaining marzipan into two, and tint black and red. To shape the chess pieces, roll 50g/2oz/4 tbsp of each colour into a sausage and cut into eight equal pieces. Shape into pawns.

5 Divide 75g/3oz/generous 4 tbsp of each colour into six equal pieces and use to shape into two castles, two knights and two bishops. (When shaping the chess pieces have a chess set to refer to so that the shapes are correct.)

6 Divide 25g/1oz/2 tbsp of each colour marzipan in half and shape a queen and a king. Decorate with silver balls. Leave to dry overnight.

7 Cut 1cm/½in black strips of marzipan to edge the board and stick in place with water. Pipe a border around the base of the cake with royal icing. Place the chess pieces in position.

Computer Game Cake

Making a cake look like a computer is easier than you think. This cake is ideal for a computer-game fanatic.

Makes one 14 x 13cm/ 5½ x 5in cake

15cm/6in square sponge cake
115g/4oz/½ cup butter icing
45ml/3 tbsp apricot jam, warmed and sieved
225g/8oz marzipan

275g/10oz/scant 2 cups sugarpaste icing
black, blue, red and yellow food colouring
royal icing, to decorate

Materials/equipment

20cm/8in square cake board
wooden cocktail stick (toothpick)
fine paintbrush
small baking parchment piping (icing) bag

1 Split the cake and fill with a little butter icing. Cut 2.5cm/1in off one side of the cake and 1cm/½in off the other side. Round the corners slightly.

2 Place the cake on the cake board and brush with apricot jam. Roll out the marzipan into a thin layer and use to cover the cake.

3 Tint 225g/8oz/1½ cups of the sugarpaste black. Use to cover the cake. Reserve the trimmings. With a cocktail stick, mark the speaker holes and position of the screen and knobs.

4 Tint half the remaining sugarpaste pale blue, roll out and cut out a 6cm/2½in square for the screen. Stick in the centre of the game with a little water.

5 Tint a small piece of sugarpaste red and the rest yellow. Use to cut out the switch and controls. Stick in position with water.

6 Roll the reserved black sugarpaste icing into a long, thin sausage and edge the screen and base of the cake.

7 With a fine paintbrush, draw the game on to the screen with a little blue colouring (choose the child's favourite game, if you like). Pipe letters on to the buttons with royal icing.

Energy 4558kcal/19093kJ; Fat 239.2g, Saturated fat 63.7g; Carbohydrate 583.9g; Fibre 10.6g

Energy 9755kcal/41011kJ; Fat 415g, Saturated fat 109.6g; Carbohydrate 1498.4g; Fibre 22.9g

Kite Cake

The happy face on this cheerful kite is a great favourite with children of all ages.

Serves 10–12
25cm/10in square sponge cake
225g/8oz/1 cup butter icing
45ml/3 tbsp apricot jam, warmed and sieved
450g/1lb marzipan
675g/1½lb/4½ cups sugarpaste icing
yellow, red, green, blue and black food colouring
115g/4oz/¾ cup royal icing

Materials/equipment
30cm/12in square cake board
wooden cocktail stick (toothpick)
small baking parchment piping (icing) bag
medium star nozzle
candles and holders

1 Trim the cake into a kite shape, then split and fill with butter icing. Place diagonally on the cake board and brush with apricot jam. Cover with a layer of marzipan.

2 Tint 225g/8oz/1½ cups of the sugarpaste icing pale yellow and cover the cake.

3 Make a template of the face, tie and buttons from baking parchment, and mark on to the cake with a cocktail stick. Divide the remainder of the sugarpaste icing into four and tint red, green, blue and black. Cut out the features and stick on with water.

4 Pipe a royal icing border around the base of the cake.

5 For the ribbons on the kite's tail, roll out each colour separately and cut two 4 x 1cm/1½ x ½in lengths in blue, red and green. Pinch each length to shape into a bow.

6 Roll the yellow sugarpaste into a long rope and lay it on the board in a wavy line from the narrow end of the kite. Stick the bows in place with water. To make the candleholders, roll balls of yellow sugarpaste, stick on the board with a little royal icing and press in the candles.

Hotdog Cake

This realistic hotdog cake is sure to be popular at a party.

Makes one 23cm/9in long cake
23 x 33cm/9 x 13in sponge roll
175g/6oz/¾ cup coffee flavour butter icing
90ml/6 tbsp apricot jam, warmed and sieved
450g/1lb/3 cups sugarpaste icing
brown and red food colouring
115g/4oz/¾ cup glacé icing
15–30ml/1–2 tbsp toasted sesame seeds

Filling
175g/6oz sponge cake pieces
50g/2oz/¼ cup soft dark brown sugar
45ml/3 tbsp orange juice
75ml/5 tbsp honey

Materials/equipment
fine paintbrush
2 small baking parchment piping (icing) bags
napkin, plate, knife and fork

1 Unroll the sponge roll, spread with butter icing, then roll up again. Slice the sponge roll along the centre lengthways, almost to the base, and ease the two halves apart.

2 Mix all the filling ingredients in a food processor or blender until smooth. Shape the mixture with your hands to a 23cm/9in sausage shape.

3 Tint all the sugarpaste icing brown. Set aside 50g/2oz/4 tbsp and use the rest to cover the cake.

4 Paint the top of the "bun" with diluted brown food colouring to give a toasted effect. Position the "sausage".

5 Divide the glacé icing in half. Tint one half brown and the other red. Pipe red icing along the sausage, then overlay with brown icing. Sprinkle the sesame seeds over the "bun".

6 Cut the reserved brown sugarpaste icing into thin strips. Place on the cake with the joins under the "sausage".

7 Place on a napkin on a serving plate, with a knife and fork.

Energy 726kcal/3054kJ; Fat 29.7g, Saturated fat 8.6g; Carbohydrate 115.2g; Fibre 1.3

Energy 4251kcal/18030kJ; Fat 73.9g, Saturated fat 11.4g; Carbohydrate 907.4g; Fibre 6g

Drum Cake

This is a colourful cake for very young children. It even comes complete with bright drumsticks.

Makes one 15cm/6in round cake

15cm/6in round sponge cake
50g/2oz/4 tbsp butter icing

45ml/3 tbsp apricot jam, warmed and sieved
350g/12oz marzipan
450g/1lb/3 cups sugarpaste icing
red, blue and yellow food colouring
royal icing, for sticking

Materials/equipment

20cm/8in round cake board

1 Split the cake and fill with a little butter icing. Place on the cake board and brush with apricot jam. Cover with a layer of marzipan and leave to dry overnight.

2 Tint half of the sugarpaste icing red and roll it out to 25 × 30cm/10 × 12in. Cut in half and stick to the side of the cake with water.

3 Roll out a circle of white sugarpaste icing to fit the top of the cake and divide the remainder in half. Tint one half blue and the other yellow.

4 Divide the blue into four pieces and roll each into a sausage long enough to go halfway round the cake. Stick around the base and top of the cake with a little water.

5 To make the drum strings, mark the cake into six around the top and base. Roll the yellow sugarpaste icing into 12 strands long enough to cross diagonally from top to base to form the drum strings. Roll the rest of the yellow icing into 12 small balls and stick at the top and base of the zigzags where the strings join the drum.

6 Knead together the red and white sugarpaste icing until streaky, then roll two balls and sticks 15cm/6in long. Leave to dry thoroughly, ideally overnight in a warm, dry place such as an airing cupboard. Stick together with royal icing to make the drumsticks and place on top of the cake.

Energy 5353kcal/22501kJ; Fat 228.2g, Saturated fat 51.4g; Carbohydrate 817.3g; Fibre 12.1g

Ice Cream Cones

Individual cakes make a change for a party. Put a candle in the special person's one.

Makes 9

115g/4oz/³⁄₄ cup marzipan
9 ice cream cones
9 sponge fairy cakes
350g/12oz/1¹⁄₂ cups butter icing

red, green and brown food colouring
coloured and chocolate vermicelli, wafers and flaked chocolate bars
sweets (candies)

Materials/equipment

3 x 12-egg egg boxes
foil

1 Make the stands for the cakes by turning the egg boxes upside down and pressing three balls of marzipan into evenly spaced holes in each box. Wrap the boxes in foil.

2 Pierce the foil above the marzipan balls and insert the cones, being careful to press them in gently so that you do not crush the bottom of the cones.

3 Gently push a fairy cake into each cone. If the bases of the cakes are too large, trim them down with a small, sharp knife. The cakes should be quite secure in the cones.

4 Divide the butter icing between three bowls and tint them pale red, green and brown.

5 Using a small metal spatula, spread each cake with some of the pink icing, making sure that the finish on the icing is a little textured so that it looks like ice cream. Use the other coloured icings in the same way for all the ice cream cones.

6 To insert a wafer or chocolate stick into an ice cream, use a small, sharp knife to make a hole through the icing and into the cake, then insert the wafer or stick.

7 Add the finishing touches to the cakes by sprinkling over some coloured and chocolate vermicelli. Arrange sweets around the cones.

Energy 576kcal/2416kJ; Fat 28.8g, Saturated fat 10.5g; Carbohydrate 78.6g; Fibre 1.1g

Royal Crown Cake

This bejewelled regal cake is sure to delight any prince or princess.

Serves 16–20

20cm/8in and 15cm/6in round sponge cake
175g/6oz/¾ cup butter icing
45ml/3 tbsp apricot jam, warmed and sieved
450g/1lb marzipan
500g/1¼lb/3¾ cups sugarpaste icing
red food colouring
450g/1lb/3 cups royal icing
small black jelly sweets (candies)
4 ice cream fan wafers
edible silver balls
jewel sweets (candies)

Materials/equipment

30cm/12in square cake board
wooden cocktail sticks (toothpicks)

1 Split the cakes and fill with butter icing. Sandwich one on top of the other and place on the cake board. Shape the top cake into a dome.

2 Brush the cake with apricot jam. Roll out the marzipan thinly and use to cover the cake. Set aside 115g/4oz/¾ cup of the sugarpaste icing and use the remainder to cover the cake.

3 Tint the reserved sugarpaste icing red, and use to cover the dome of the cake. Trim away the excess.

4 Spoon rough mounds of royal icing around the base of the cake and stick a black jelly sweet on each mound.

5 Cut the ice cream wafers diagonally in half. Spread both sides of the wafers with royal icing and stick to the cake to form the points of the crown, smoothing the icing level with the sides of the cake.

6 Use cocktail sticks to support the wafers until they are dry.

7 Position silver balls on top of each point and stick jewel sweets around the side of the crown using a little royal icing to stick them securely.

Treasure Map

Perhaps you could combine this map with a treasure hunt at the party.

Makes one 20 x 25cm/ 8 x 10in cake

25cm/10in square sponge cake
225g/8oz/1½ cups butter icing
45ml/3 tbsp apricot jam, warmed and sieved
450g/1lb/3 cups marzipan
675g/1½lb/4½ cups sugarpaste icing
yellow, brown, paprika, green, black and red food colouring
115g/4oz/¾ cup royal icing

Materials/equipment

25 x 35cm/10 x 14in cake board
fine paintbrush
kitchen paper
4 small baking parchment piping (icing) bags
medium shell and fine writing nozzles
candles and holders

1 Split the cake and fill with butter icing, cut it into a 20 x 25cm/8 x 10in rectangle and place on the cake board. Brush with apricot jam. Cover with a layer of marzipan then with 450g/1lb/3 cups sugarpaste icing.

2 Colour the remaining sugarpaste icing yellow and cut out with an uneven outline. Stick on to the cake with water and leave to dry overnight. Mark the island, river, lake, mountains and trees on the map.

3 With brown and paprika colours and a fine paintbrush, paint the edges of the map to look old, smudging the colours together with kitchen paper.

4 Paint the island pale green and the water around the island, the river and the lake pale blue. Dry overnight before painting on the other details, otherwise the colours will run.

5 Pipe a border of royal icing around the base of the cake with the shell nozzle. Colour a little royal icing red and pipe the path to the treasure, marked with an "X", with the writing nozzle.

6 Colour some icing green and pipe on grass and trees. Colour some icing black and pipe on a north sign with the writing nozzle.

Energy 8201kcal/34461kJ; Fat 356.9g, Saturated fat 103.1g; Carbohydrate 1246.5g; Fibre 15.8g

Energy 427kcal/1798kJ; Fat 16.5g, Saturated fat 4.9g; Carbohydrate 70.4g; Fibre 0.7g

Box of Chocolates Cake

This sophisticated cake is perfect for an older child's birthday and will delight chocolate lovers.

Makes one 15cm/6in square cake

15cm/6in square
   sponge cake
50g/2oz/4 tbsp butter icing
30ml/2 tbsp apricot jam, warmed
   and sieved

350g/12oz marzipan
350g/12oz/2¼ cups
   sugarpaste icing
red food colouring
wrapped chocolates

Materials/equipment

20cm/8in square cake board
small paper sweet
   (candy) cases
1.35m/1½yd x 4cm/1½in-wide
   gold and red ribbon

1 Split the cake in half and sandwich together with butter icing. Cut a shallow square from the top of the cake, leaving a 1cm/¼in border around the edge.

2 Place on the cake board and brush with apricot jam. Cover with a layer of marzipan.

3 Roll out the sugarpaste icing and cut an 18cm/7in square. Ease it into the hollow dip and trim. Tint the remaining sugarpaste icing red and use to cover the sides.

4 Put the chocolates into paper cases and arrange in the box. Tie the ribbon around the sides with a big bow.

Cook's Tip

If you often make cakes using sugarpaste it is worth investing in a smoother. This is a flat plastic tool with a handle, and it is useful for achieving a professional finish. Use the smoother to smooth the sugarpaste over the top of the cake, using your hand to finish rounded edges. Then push the smoother down the sides of the cake and press the edge along the base where the sugarpaste meets the board. This will give a neat edge for you to cut away with a knife.

Strawberry Cake

Use a heart-shaped mould or cut a round cake to shape using a template for this cake.

Makes one 900g/2lb cake

650g/1lb 7oz/scant 4½ cups
   marzipan
green, red and yellow
   food colouring

30ml/2 tbsp apricot jam, warmed
   and sieved
900g/2lb heart-shaped sponge cake
caster (superfine) sugar,
   for dusting

Materials/equipment

30cm/12in round
   cake board
icing smoother

1 Tint 175g/6oz/generous 1 cup of the marzipan green. Brush the cake board with apricot jam, roll out the green marzipan and use to cover the board. Trim the edges. Use an icing smoother to flatten and smooth the marzipan.

2 Brush the remaining apricot jam over the top and sides of the cake. Position the cake on the cake board. Tint 275g/10oz/scant 2 cups of the remaining marzipan red. Roll it out to 5mm/¼in thick and use to cover the cake, smoothing down the sides. Trim the edges. Use the handle of a teaspoon to indent the "strawberry" evenly and lightly all over.

3 For the stalk, tint 175g/6oz/generous 1 cup of the marzipan bright green. Cut it in half and roll out one portion into a 10 x 15cm/4 x 6in rectangle. Cut "V" shapes out of the rectangle, leaving a 2.5cm/1in border across the top, to form the calyx. Position on the cake, curling the "V" shapes to make them look realistic.

4 Roll the rest of the green marzipan into a sausage shape 13cm/5in long. Bend it slightly, then position it on the board to form the stalk.

5 For the strawberry pips, tint the remaining marzipan yellow. Pull off tiny pieces and roll them into tear-shaped pips. Place them in the indentations all over the strawberry. Dust the cake and board with sifted caster sugar.

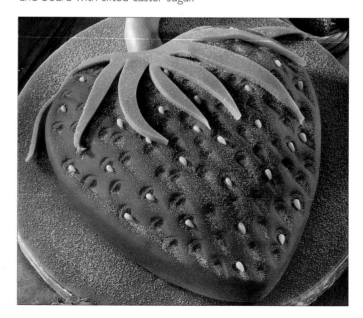

Energy 4150kcal/17538kJ; Fat 123g, Saturated fat 46.5g; Carbohydrate 762.1g; Fibre 6.7g

Energy 6810kcal/28566kJ; Fat 327.4g, Saturated fat 58.9g; Carbohydrate 931.7g; Fibre 20.4g

Gift-wrapped Parcel

If you don't have a tiny flower cutter for the "wrapping paper" design, then press a small decorative button into the icing while still soft to create a pattern.

Makes one 15cm/6in square cake
15cm/6in square cake
50g/2oz/4 tbsp butter icing
45ml/3 tbsp apricot jam, warmed and sieved
450g/1lb marzipan
350g/12oz/2¼ cups pale lemon yellow sugarpaste icing
red and green food colouring
30ml/2 tbsp royal icing

Materials/equipment
20cm/8in square cake board
small flower cutter (optional)

1 Split the cake and fill with butter icing. Place on the cake board and brush with the warmed apricot jam. Cover with half the marzipan, then with the yellow sugarpaste icing, and mark with a small flower cutter.

2 To make the ribbons divide the remaining marzipan in half, and colour one half pink and the other pale green. Roll out the pink marzipan and cut into four 2.5 x 18cm/1 x 7in strips. Roll out the green marzipan and cut into four 1cm/½in strips the same length.

3 Centre the green strips on top of the pink strips and stick on to the cake with a little water. Cut two 5cm/2in strips from each colour and cut a "V" from the ends to form the ends of the ribbon. Stick in place and leave to dry overnight.

4 Cut the rest of the green into four 2.5 x 7.5cm/1 x 3in lengths and the pink into four 1 x 7.5cm/½ x 3in lengths. Centre the pink on top of the green, fold in half, stick the ends together and slip over the handle of a wooden spoon, dusted with cornflour. Leave to dry overnight.

5 Cut the ends into "V" shapes to fit neatly together on the cake. Cut two pieces for the join in the centre. Remove the bows from the spoon and stick in position with royal icing.

Energy 5031kcal/21295kJ; Fat 116.3g, Saturated fat 36g; Carbohydrate 992g; Fibre 8.6g

Sweetheart Cake

The heart-shaped run-outs can be made a week before the cake is made to ensure that they are completely dry.

Makes one 20cm/8in round cake
20cm/8in round sponge cake
115g/4oz/½ cup butter icing
45ml/3 tbsp apricot jam, warmed and served
450g/1lb marzipan

675g/1½lb/4½ cups sugarpaste icing
red food colouring
115g/4oz/¾ cup royal icing

Materials/equipment
25cm/10in round cake board
spoon with decorative handle
small baking parchment piping (icing) bag
no.1 writing nozzle
candles and holders
1.5m/1½yd x 2.5cm/1in wide ribbon

1 Split the cake and fill with butter icing. Place on the cake board and brush with apricot jam. Cover with a layer of marzipan. Tint the sugarpaste icing pale pink and cover the cake and board. Mark the edge of the icing with the decorative handle of a spoon.

2 Tint the royal icing dark pink. Make a heart-shaped template and draw round this several times on a sheet of baking parchment. Using a no.1 writing nozzle, pipe the outlines for the hearts in a continuous line. Then fill in until the hearts are rounded. You will need eight for the cake top. Make some extra in case of mistakes. Leave to dry for at least 2 days.

3 Arrange the hearts on top of the cake and place the candles in the centre. Tie the ribbon around the cake.

Cook's Tip
When using royal icing to create shapes such as these hearts, make sure that it is the correct consistency. If it is too thin the icing will overflow the edge of the shape; if it is too thick it will form a lumpy surface. Always make several more shapes than you need in case any are damaged when you transfer them from the paper to the cake.

Energy 7060kcal/29760kJ; Fat 245g, Saturated fat 55.1g; Carbohydrate 1224.6g; Fibre 14g

Rosette Cake

This impressive cake could be used for a Christening or anniversary party.

Makes one 20cm/8in square cake

20cm/8in square sponge cake
450g/1lb/2 cups butter icing
60ml/4 tbsp apricot jam, warmed and sieved

mulberry-red food colouring
crystallized violets

Materials/equipment

25cm/10in square cake board
serrated scraper
piping (icing) bag
large star nozzle
candles and holders

1 Split the cake and fill with a little butter icing. Place in the centre of the cake board and brush with apricot jam. Tint the remaining butter icing dark pink using the mulberry-red food colouring. Spread the top and sides with butter icing.

2 Using the serrated scraper, hold it against the cake and move it from side to side across the top to make waves. Hold the scraper against the side of the cake, resting the flat edge on the board, and draw it along to give straight ridges along each side.

3 Put the rest of the butter icing into a piping bag fitted with a large star nozzle. Mark a 15cm/6in circle on the top of the cake and pipe stars around it and around the base of the cake. Place the candles and violets in the corners.

Cook's Tip
So that you have perfect little stars for your cake, practise piping icing on to a plate beforehand. Make sure there is no air in the icing by twisting the top of the bag and then squeezing a little icing out before you start. Hold the twist between the joint of the thumb and first finger and hold the bag in the palm of your hand. Hold the piping (icing) bag with the star nozzle directly over and close to the surface to be iced. Squeeze out some icing while gently pushing downwards and then move the icing bag upwards without squeezing to form a point.

Number 10 Cake

Ideal as a birthday or anniversary cake, this is a very simple cake to decorate. If you can't master the shell edge, pipe stars instead.

Makes one 20cm/8in tall round cake

20cm/8in and 15cm/6in round sponge cakes
450g/1lb/2 cups butter icing
75ml/5 tbsp apricot jam, warmed and sieved

coloured vermicelli
cream food colouring

Materials/equipment

25cm/10in round cake board
wooden cocktail stick (toothpick)
plastic "10" cake decoration
small baking parchment piping (icing) bag
thick shell and star nozzles
10 candles and holders

1 Split both cakes and fill with a little butter icing. Brush the sides with the warmed apricot jam.

2 When the jam is cold, spread a layer of butter icing over the sides and then roll in coloured vermicelli to cover evenly.

3 Tint the rest of the icing cream, and spread over the top of each cake. Place the small cake on top of the large cake. Using a cocktail stick, make a pattern in the icing on top of the cake.

4 Using the remaining icing, pipe around the base of the cakes and around the edge. Stick the "10" decoration in the centre of the top tier and two candles on either side. Arrange the other candles evenly around the base cake.

Cook's Tip
To pipe shells, hold the piping bag at an angle and close to the surface to be iced and gently squeeze out some of the icing while you move the bag gently slightly upwards and away from you then towards you to make a tiny loop. Let the icing touch the surface a fraction behind the loop and continue as before. Practise on a plate before you ice the cake.

Glittering Star Cake

With a quick flick of a paintbrush you can give a sparkling effect to this glittering cake. Sparkle and glitter food colours make a cake very special.

Makes one 20cm/8in round cake

20cm/8in round rich fruit cake
40ml/2½ tbsp apricot jam, warmed and sieved

675g/1½lb/4½ cups marzipan
450g/1lb/3 cups sugarpaste icing
115g/4oz/¾ cup royal icing
silver, gold, lilac shimmer, red sparkle, glitter green and primrose sparkle food colouring and powder tints

Materials/equipment
paintbrush
25cm/10in round cake board

1 Brush the cake with the apricot jam. Use two-thirds of the marzipan to cover the cake. Leave to dry overnight.

2 Cover the cake with the sugarpaste icing. Leave to dry.

3 Place the cake on a large sheet of baking parchment. Dilute a little powdered silver food colouring and, using a loaded paintbrush, flick it all over the cake to give a spattered effect. Allow to dry.

4 Make templates of two different-size moon shapes and three irregular star shapes.

5 Divide the remaining marzipan into six pieces and tint them silver, gold, lilac, pink, green and yellow. Cut the coloured sugarpaste into stars and moons using the templates as a guide, cutting some of the stars in half.

6 Place the cut-outs on baking parchment and brush each with its own colour powder tint. Allow to dry.

7 Secure the cake on the board with royal icing. Arrange the marzipan stars and moons at different angles all over the cake, attaching with royal icing, and position the halved stars upright as though coming out of the cake. Allow to set.

Energy 7800kcal/33013kJ; Fat 159.5g, Saturated fat 28.6g; Carbohydrate 1548.9g; Fibre 26.3g

Racing Ring Cake

Liquorice makes simple but effective tracks for brightly coloured cars.

Serves 12
ring mould sponge cake
350g/12oz/1½ cups butter icing
500g/1¼lb/3¾ cups sugarpaste icing
125g/4oz/¾ cup royal icing, for fixing
black, blue, yellow, green, orange, red, purple food colouring

selection of liquorice sweets (candies), dolly mixtures and teddy bears
113g/4½oz packet liquorice Catherine wheels

Materials/equipment
25cm/10in round cake board
wooden kebab skewer
fine paintbrush

1 Cut the cake in half horizontally and fill with some butter icing. Cover the outside with the remaining butter icing.

2 Use 350g/12oz/2¼ cups of sugarpaste icing to coat the top and inside of the cake. Use the trimmings to roll an oblong for the flag. Cut the skewer to 13cm/5in and fold one end of the flag around it, securing with water. Paint on the pattern with black food colouring. Colour a ball of icing black, and stick on top of the skewer. Make a few folds in the flag and leave to dry.

3 Colour the remaining sugarpaste icing blue, yellow, green, orange, red and a very small amount purple. Shape each car in two pieces, attaching in the centre with royal icing where the seat joins the body of the car. Add decorations and headlights and attach dolly mixture wheels with royal icing. Place a teddy bear in each car and leave to set.

4 Unwind the Catherine wheels and remove the centre sweets. Fix them to the top of the cake with royal icing. Secure one strip around the bottom. Cut some of the liquorice into small strips and attach around the middle of the outside of the cake with royal icing. Arrange small liquorice sweets around the bottom of the cake. Position the cars on top of the cake on the tracks and attach the flag to the outside with royal icing.

Energy 622kcal/2603kJ; Fat 34.3g, Saturated fat 13.2g; Carbohydrate 77.8g; Fibre 0.8g

Artist's Cake

Making cakes is an art in itself, and this cake proves it! Take your time to model the handle and catches for the box for the best effect.

Makes one 20cm/8in square cake

20cm/8in square rich fruit cake
45ml/3 tbsp apricot jam, warmed and sieved

450g/1lb marzipan
800g/1¾lb/5¼ cups sugarpaste icing
chestnut, yellow, blue, black, silver, paprika, green and mulberry food colouring
115g/4oz/¾ cup royal icing

Materials/equipment

25cm/10in square cake board
fine paintbrush

1 Brush the cake with the apricot jam. Cover in marzipan and leave to dry overnight.

2 Make a template of a painter's palette that will fit the cake top. Tint 175g/6oz/generous 1 cup of the sugarpaste very pale chestnut. Cut out the palette shape, place on baking parchment and leave to dry overnight.

3 Tint 450g/1lb/3 cups of the sugarpaste icing dark chestnut. Use to cover the cake. Secure the cake on the board with royal icing. Leave to dry.

4 Divide half the remaining sugarpaste icing into seven equal parts and tint yellow, blue, black, silver, paprika, green and mulberry.

5 Make all the decorative pieces for the box and palette, using the remaining white sugarpaste for the paint tubes.

6 Leave all the decorative pieces to dry on baking parchment.

7 Paint black markings on the paint tubes and chestnut wood markings on the box.

8 Position all the sugarpaste pieces on the cake and board using royal icing. Leave to dry.

Energy 7370kcal/31233kJ; Fat 122.8g, Saturated fat 23.8g; Carbohydrate 1546g; Fibre 20.6g

"Liquorice" Cake

Scaled-up versions of favourite sweets (candies) make a great decoration for a cake.

Makes one 20cm/8in square cake

20cm/8in and 15cm/6in square Madeira cakes
675g/1½lb/3 cups butter icing
45ml/3 tbsp apricot jam, warmed and sieved

350g/12oz marzipan
800g/1¾lb/5¼ cups sugarpaste icing
egg-yellow, black, blue and mulberry food colouring

Materials/equipment

25cm/10in square cake board
4.5cm/1¾in round cutter

1 Cut both cakes horizontally into three. Fill with butter icing, reserving a little to coat the smaller cake. Wrap and set aside the smaller cake. Brush the larger cake with apricot jam. Cover with marzipan and secure on the cake board with butter icing. Leave to dry overnight.

2 Tint 350g/12oz/2¼ cups of the sugarpaste icing yellow. Take 115g/4oz/¾ cup of the remaining sugarpaste icing and tint half black and leave the other half white. Cover the top and one-third of the sides of the cake with yellow sugarpaste icing.

3 Use the white icing to cover the lower third of the sides of the cake. Use the black icing to fill the central third.

4 Cut the smaller cake into three equal strips. Divide two of the strips into three squares each. Cut out two circles from the third strip, using a cutter as a guide.

5 Tint 115g/4oz/¾ cup of the remaining sugarpaste black. Divide the rest into four equal portions; leave one white and tint the others blue, pink and yellow.

6 Coat the outsides of the cake cut-outs with the reserved butter icing. Use the tinted and white sugarpaste to cover the pieces to resemble liquorice sweets (candies). Make small rolls from the trimmings. Arrange on and around the cake.

Energy 9108kcal/38287kJ; Fat 396.8g, Saturated fat 218.9g; Carbohydrate 1409.7g; Fibre 12.9g

Sun Cake

This smiling sun is very easy to make from two round cakes with a quickly piped icing design.

Makes one 20cm/8in star-shaped cake

2 sponge cakes, 20 x 5cm/
   8 x 2in each
25g/1oz/2 tbsp unsalted
   (sweet) butter
450g/1lb/4 cups sifted icing
   (confectioners') sugar
120ml/4fl oz/¹/₂ cup
   apricot jam
30ml/2 tbsp water
2 large (US extra large)
   egg whites
1–2 drops glycerine
juice of 1 lemon
yellow and orange
   food colouring

Materials/equipment
40cm/16in square
   cake board
fabric piping (icing) bag
small star nozzle

1 Cut one of the cakes into eight wedges. Trim the outsides to fit around the other cake.

2 To make the butter icing, combine the butter with 25g/1oz/ 2 tbsp of the icing sugar.

3 Place the whole cake on a 40cm/16in board and attach the sunbeams with the butter icing.

4 Warm the jam with the water in a small bowl set over a pan of simmering water. Brush the jam all over the cake.

5 For the icing, beat the egg whites until they are stiff. Gradually add the icing sugar, glycerine and lemon juice, and beat together for 1 minute.

6 Tint three-quarters of the icing yellow and spread it all over the cake.

7 Tint the remaining icing bright yellow and orange.

8 Pipe the details on to the cake with the small star nozzle.

Energy 7899kcal/33176kJ; Fat 346.9g, Saturated fat 82.6g; Carbohydrate 1182g; Fibre 10.8g

Strawberry Basket Cake

For a summer birthday what could be nicer than a basket full of strawberries?

Makes one small rectangular cake
sponge cake baked in a 450g/
   1lb/3 cup loaf tin (pan)
45ml/3 tbsp apricot jam, warmed
   and sieved
675g/1¹/₂lb marzipan
350g/12oz/1¹/₂ cups chocolate-
   flavour butter icing
red food colouring
50g/2oz/¹/₄ cup caster
   (superfine) sugar

Materials/equipment
small star nozzle
small baking parchment piping
   (icing) bag
10 plastic strawberry stalks
30 x 7.5cm/12 x 3in strip foil
30cm/12in thin red ribbon

1 Level the top of the cake and make it perfectly flat. Score a 5mm/¹/₄in border around the edge and scoop out the inside to make a shallow hollow.

2 Brush the sides and border edges of the cake with apricot jam. Roll out 275g/10oz/scant 2 cups of the marzipan, cut into rectangles and use to cover the sides of the cake, overlapping the borders. Press the edges together to seal.

3 Using the star nozzle and the butter icing, pipe vertical lines 2.5cm/1in apart all around the sides of the cake. Pipe short horizontal lines of butter icing alternately crossing over and then stopping at the vertical lines to give a basketweave effect. Pipe a decorative line of icing around the top edge of the basket to finish.

4 Tint the remaining marzipan red and mould it into ten strawberry shapes. Roll in the caster sugar and press a plastic strawberry calyx into each top. Arrange in the "basket".

5 For the basket handle, fold the foil into a thin strip and wind the ribbon around it to cover. Bend up the ends and then bend into a curve. Push the ends into the sides of the cake. Decorate with bows made from the ribbon.

Energy 6807kcal/28601kJ; Fat 303.9g, Saturated fat 88g; Carbohydrate 1011.2g; Fibre 17.3g

Individual Brioches

These buttery rolls with their distinctive topknots are delicious served with strawberry jam.

Makes 8
15ml/1 tbsp active dried yeast
15ml/1 tbsp caster (superfine) sugar
30ml/2 tbsp warm milk
2 eggs
about 200g/7oz/1¾ cups strong white bread flour
2.5ml/½ tsp salt
75g/3oz/6 tbsp butter, cut into six pieces, at room temperature
1 egg yolk, beaten with 10ml/ 2 tsp water, to glaze

1 Butter eight individual brioche tins (pans) or muffin cups. Put the yeast and sugar in a small bowl, add the milk and stir until dissolved. Leave the yeast mixture to stand for 5 minutes so that the yeast begins to work, then beat in the eggs.

2 Put the flour and salt into a food processor, then, with the machine running, slowly pour in the yeast mixture. Scrape down the sides and process until the dough forms a ball.

3 Add the butter and pulse to blend. Alternatively, use your hand to incorporate the flour into the liquid.

4 Transfer the dough to a lightly buttered bowl and cover with a clean dish towel or clear film (plastic wrap). Leave to rise in a warm place for about 1 hour, then knock back (punch down) the dough.

5 Shape three-quarters of the dough into eight balls and place them into the prepared tins. Shape the last quarter into eight small balls, make a depression in the top of each large ball and set a small ball into it.

6 Leave the brioches to rise in a warm place for 30 minutes. Preheat the oven to 200°C/400°F/Gas 6.

7 Brush the brioches with the egg glaze. Bake for about 15–18 minutes, or until golden brown. Transfer to a wire rack and leave to cool completely.

Milk Rolls

These bread rolls are not only delicious, but they are quite easy to make too.

Makes 12–16
750g/1lb 10oz/6½ cups strong white bread flour
10ml/2 tsp salt
25g/1oz/2 tbsp butter
1 sachet easy-blend (rapid-rise) dried yeast
450ml/¾ pint/1¾ cups lukewarm milk
cold milk, to glaze
poppy, sesame and sunflower seeds, or sea salt flakes, for sprinkling

1 Sift together the flour and salt into a large bowl. Rub in the butter, then stir in the yeast. Mix to a firm dough with the lukewarm milk (you may not need it all).

2 Knead the dough for 5 minutes on a lightly floured surface, then return it to the bowl, cover with a clean dish towel or clear film (plastic wrap), and leave to rise until doubled in volume, about 1½ hours.

3 Grease a baking sheet. Knock back (punch down) the dough and knead again, then divide into 12–16 pieces and form into shapes of your choice.

4 You can make mini-cottage loaves by setting a small ball on to a larger one and pressing a finger in the top; use three lengths of dough to make a braid; one long length can be made into a simple knot; or make three cuts in a round roll for an easier decoration.

5 Place the rolls or mini-cottage loaves on the baking sheet, glaze the tops with milk, and sprinkle over your chosen seeds or sea salt flakes.

6 Leave in a warm place to start rising again. Meanwhile, preheat the oven to 230°C/450°F/Gas 8. Bake the rolls for 12 minutes, or until golden brown and cooked. Turn out on to a wire rack. and leave to cool. (Eat the rolls the same day as they will not keep well.)

Energy 183kcal/765kJ; Fat 9.5g, Saturated fat 5.4g; Carbohydrate 21.6g; Fibre 0.8g

Energy 247kcal/1047kJ; Fat 3.2g, Saturated fat 1.6g; Carbohydrate 50.4g; Fibre 1.9g

Pleated Rolls

The odd shapes of these rolls will add to their interest for children.

Makes 48 rolls
15ml/1 tbsp active dried yeast
475ml/16fl oz/2 cups
   lukewarm milk
115g/4oz/½ cup margarine
50g/2oz/¼ cup caster
   (superfine) sugar
10ml/2 tsp salt
2 eggs
985g–1.2kg/2lb 3oz–2½lb/
   scant 7–8 cups strong white
   bread flour
50g/2oz/¼ cup butter

1 Combine the yeast and 120ml/4fl oz/½ cup milk in a large bowl. Stir and leave for 15 minutes. Scald the remaining milk, leave to cool for 5 minutes, then beat in the margarine, sugar, salt and eggs. Leave until lukewarm.

2 Pour the milk mixture into the yeast mixture. Stir in half the flour with a wooden spoon. Add the remaining flour, 150g/5oz/1¼ cups at a time, to obtain a rough dough.

3 Transfer the dough to a floured surface and knead until elastic. This will take about 10 minutes. Place in a clean bowl, cover with clear film (plastic wrap) and leave to rise in a warm place until doubled in volume. Melt the butter and set aside.

4 Lightly grease two baking sheets. Knock back (punch down) the dough and divide into four equal pieces. Roll each piece into a 30 × 20cm/12 × 8in rectangle, about 5mm/¼in thick. Cut each of the rectangles into four long strips, then cut each strip into three 10 × 5cm/4 × 2in rectangles.

5 Brush each rectangle with the melted butter, then fold the rectangles in half, so that the top extends about 1cm/½in over the bottom. Place the rectangles slightly overlapping on the baking sheet, with the longer sides facing up.

6 Cover and chill for 30 minutes. Preheat the oven to 180°C/350°F/Gas 4. Bake until golden, 18–20 minutes. Cool slightly before serving.

Energy 107kcal/452kJ; Fat 3.5g, Saturated 0.8g; Carbohydrate 17.5g; Fibre 0.6g

Clover Leaf Rolls

These rolls are delightful for any occasion. For a witty touch, make one "lucky four-leaf clover" in the batch.

Makes 24
300ml/½ pint/1¼ cups milk
30ml/2 tbsp caster
   (superfine) sugar
50g/2oz/¼ cup butter,
   at room temperature
10ml/2 tsp active dried yeast
1 egg
10ml/2 tsp salt
450–500g/1–1¼lb/4–5 cups
   strong white bread flour
melted butter, to glaze

1 Heat the milk to lukewarm in a small pan, pour into a large bowl and stir in the sugar, butter and yeast. Leave for 15 minutes to dissolve and for the yeast to become frothy.

2 Stir the egg and salt into the yeast mixture. Gradually stir in 475g/1lb 2oz/4½ cups of the flour, and then add just enough extra flour to obtain a rough dough.

3 Knead the dough on a lightly floured surface until smooth. This will take about 10 minutes.

4 Place the dough in a greased bowl, cover with clear film (plastic wrap) and leave in a warm place until doubled in size, about 1½ hours.

5 Grease two 12-cup bun trays. Knock back (punch down) the dough, and divide to make 72 equal-size balls.

6 Place three balls, in one layer, in each bun cup. Cover the trays loosely with a clean dish towel and leave to rise in a warm place, until doubled in size, about 1½ hours.

7 Meanwhile, preheat the oven to 200°C/400°F/Gas 6. Brush the rolls with the melted butter glaze.

8 Bake the rolls for about 20 minutes, or until they are lightly browned. Carefully turn out on to a wire rack and allow to cool slightly before serving.

Energy 2125kcal/8967kJ; Fat 59.8g, Saturated fat 36.1g; Carbohydrate 342.2g; Fibre 13.2g

Two-tone Bread

A tasty, malty bread that, when cut, reveals an attractive swirled interior.

Makes two 350g/12oz loaves

25ml/1½ tbsp active dried yeast
120ml/4fl oz/½ cup warm water
55g/2¼oz/generous ¼ cup
    caster (superfine) sugar
675g/1½lb/6 cups strong white

bread flour
7.5ml/1½ tsp salt
600ml/1 pint/2½ cups warm milk
65g/2½oz/5 tbsp butter or
    margarine, melted and cooled
45ml/3 tbsp black treacle
    (molasses)
275g/10oz/2½ cups strong
    wholemeal (whole-wheat)
    bread flour

1 In a small bowl, dissolve the yeast in the water with 5ml/1 tsp of the sugar. Sift 350g/12oz/3 cups of the white bread flour, the salt and remaining sugar. Make a well in the centre and add the yeast, milk and butter or margarine. Mix in gradually to form a smooth soft batter.

2 Divide the batter into two bowls. To one bowl, add 275g/10oz/2½ cups of the strong white flour and mix together to a soft dough. Knead until smooth. This will take about 10 minutes. Shape into a ball, put into a greased bowl and rotate to grease all over. Cover with clear film (plastic wrap).

3 Mix the treacle and wholemeal flour into the second bowl. Add enough of the remaining white flour to make a soft dough. Knead until smooth. Shape into a ball, put in a greased bowl and cover with oiled clear film. Leave the doughs to rise in a warm place for about 1 hour, or until doubled in size. Grease two 22 x 11cm/ 8½ x 4½in loaf tins (pans).

4 Preheat the oven to 220°C/425°F/Gas 7. Knock back (punch down) the dough and divide each ball in half. Roll out half of the light dough to a 30 x 20cm/12 x 8in rectangle. Roll out half of the dark dough to the same size. Set the dark dough rectangle on the light one. Roll up tightly from a short side. Set in a loaf tin. Repeat for the other loaf. Cover the tins and leave the dough to rise until doubled in size. Bake for 30–35 minutes.

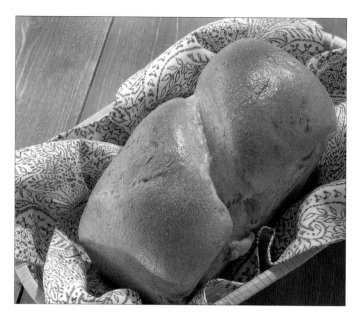

Cheese Bread

This flavoured bread is ideal for making tomato or cress sandwiches.

Makes one 23 x 13cm/ 9 x 5in loaf

15ml/1 tbsp active dried yeast
250ml/8fl oz/1 cup
    lukewarm milk

25g/1oz/2 tbsp butter
425g/15oz/3⅔ cups strong white
    bread flour
10ml/2 tsp salt
90g/3½oz/scant 1 cup grated
    mature (sharp) Cheddar cheese

1 Combine the yeast and milk in a small bowl. Stir and leave for 15 minutes to dissolve and for the yeast to become frothy.

2 Meanwhile, melt the butter, leave to cool, then add it to the yeast mixture.

3 Mix the flour and salt together in a large bowl. Make a central well in the flour and pour in the yeast mixture. With a wooden spoon, stir from the centre to obtain a rough dough. If the dough seems too dry, add 30–45ml/2–3 tbsp water.

4 Transfer to a floured surface and knead until smooth and elastic. This will take about 10 minutes. Return to the bowl, cover and leave to rise in a warm place until doubled in volume, about 2–3 hours.

5 Grease a 23 x 13cm/9 x 5in loaf tin (pan). Knock back (punch down) the dough and knead in the cheese to distribute it evenly.

6 Twist the dough, form into a loaf shape and place in the tin, tucking the ends underneath. Leave in a warm place until the dough rises above the rim of the tin, about 1½ hours.

7 Meanwhile, preheat the oven to 200°C/400°F/Gas 6. Bake the bread for 15 minutes, then lower the heat to 190°C/375°F/ Gas 5 and bake until the base sounds hollow when tapped, about a further 30 minutes.

Energy 2123kcal/8994kJ; Fat 39.3g, Saturated fat 20.8g; Carbohydrate 408.3g; Fibre 22.9g

Energy 93kcal/394kJ; Fat 2.4g, Saturated fat 1.3g; Carbohydrate 16.5g; Fibre 0.6g

Raisin Bread

Enjoy this spread with butter or honey.

Makes 2 loaves

15ml/1 tbsp active dried yeast
450ml/¾ pint/1¾ cups
  lukewarm milk
150g/5oz/1 cup raisins
65g/2½oz/½ cup currants
15ml/1 tbsp orange juice
2.5ml/½ tsp freshly grated nutmeg

grated rind of 1 large orange
60g/2¼oz/generous ¼ cup
  caster (superfine) sugar
15ml/1 tbsp salt
115g/4oz/½ cup butter, melted
700–850g/1lb 8oz–1lb 14oz/
  6–7½ cups strong white
  bread flour
1 egg beaten with 15ml/1 tbsp
  single (light) cream, to glaze

1 Stir the yeast with 120ml/4fl oz/½ cup of the milk and leave to stand for 15 minutes to dissolve. Mix the raisins, currants, orange juice, nutmeg and orange rind together.

2 In another bowl, mix the remaining milk, sugar, salt and half the butter. Add the yeast mixture. With a wooden spoon, stir in half the flour, 150g/5oz at a time, until blended. Add the remaining flour as needed to form a stiff dough. Transfer to a floured surface and knead until smooth and elastic. This will take about 10 minutes. Place in a greased bowl, cover and leave to rise in a warm place until doubled in volume, about 2½ hours.

3 Knock back (punch down) the dough, return to the bowl, cover and leave to rise in a warm place for 30 minutes. Grease two 21 × 11cm/8½ × 4½in loaf tins (pans). Divide the dough in half and roll each half into a 50 × 18cm/20 × 7in rectangle.

4 Brush the rectangles with the remaining melted butter. Sprinkle over the raisin mixture, then roll up tightly, tucking in the ends slightly as you roll. Place in the prepared tins, cover, and leave to rise until almost doubled in volume, about 1 hour. Preheat the oven to 200°C/400°F/Gas 6. Brush the loaves with the egg glaze. Bake for 20 minutes. Lower to 180°C/350°F/Gas 4 and bake until golden, 25–30 minutes more. Cool on racks.

Coconut Bread

This bread makes a delicious snack or treat at any time of the day.

Makes 1 loaf

175g/6oz/¾ cup butter
115g/4oz/½ cup demerara
  (raw) sugar
225g/8oz/2 cups self-raising
  (self-rising) flour
200g/7oz/1¾ cups plain
  (all-purpose) flour
5ml/1 tsp mixed (apple pie) spice

115g/4oz/1⅓ cups desiccated
  (dry unsweetened
  shredded) coconut
10ml/2 tsp vanilla extract
2 eggs
about 150ml/¼ pint/⅔
  cup milk
15ml/1 tbsp caster (superfine)
  sugar, blended with 30ml/
  2 tbsp water, to glaze

1 Preheat the oven to 180°C/350°F/Gas 4. Grease two 450g/1lb loaf tins (pans).

2 Place the butter and sugar in a large bowl and sift in the flour. Rub the ingredients together using your fingertips or a pastry cutter until the mixture resembles fine breadcrumbs.

3 Add the coconut, mixed spice, vanilla extract, eggs and milk to the butter and sugar mixture, and mix together well with your hands. If you think that the mixture is too dry, moisten with milk. Turn out on to a floured board and knead until firm and pliable.

4 Halve the mixture and place in the prepared loaf tins. Glaze with sugared water and bake for 1 hour, or until the loaves are cooked. Test with a skewer; the loaves are ready when the skewer comes out clean.

> **Cook's Tips**
> If you like, you can sprinkle extra coconut or other flaked nuts on top of the loaf, for decoration. It is delicious spread with butter or a fruit preserve.

Energy 2187kcal/9239kJ; Fat 58.9g, Saturated fat 33.9g; Carbohydrate 388.3g; Fibre 13g

Energy 4148kcal/17357kJ; Fat 234.3g, Saturated fat 158.1g; Carbohydrate 465.9g; Fibre 28.9g

Fruity Teabread

Serve this bread thinly sliced, toasted or plain, with butter or cream cheese and home-made jam.

Makes one 23 x 13cm/ 9 x 5in loaf
225g/8oz/2 cups plain (all-purpose) flour
115g/4oz/generous ½ cup caster (superfine) sugar
15ml/1 tbsp baking powder
2.5ml/½ tsp salt
grated rind of 1 large orange
160ml/5½fl oz/generous ⅔ cup fresh orange juice
2 eggs, lightly beaten
75g/3oz/6 tbsp butter or margarine, melted
115g/4oz/1 cup fresh cranberries or bilberries
50g/2oz/½ cup chopped walnuts

1 Preheat the oven to 180°C/350°F/Gas 4. Then line a 23 x 13cm/9 x 5in loaf tin (pan) with baking parchment and grease the paper.

2 Sift the flour, sugar, baking powder and salt into a mixing bowl. Then stir in the orange rind.

3 Make a well in the centre and add the fresh orange juice, eggs and melted butter or margarine. Stir from the centre until the ingredients are blended; do not overmix. Add the berries and walnuts, and stir until blended.

4 Transfer the mixture to the prepared tin and bake until a skewer inserted in the centre of the loaf comes out clean, about 45–50 minutes. Leave to cool in the tin for 10 minutes before transferring to a wire rack to cool completely.

Cook's Tip
Margarine can be used instead of butter for most recipes except those with a high fat content such as shortbread. Margarine will not, however, produce the same flavour as butter but it is usually less expensive so can be useful. Block margarines are better for teabreads, buns and muffins than soft margarines.

Date and Pecan Loaf

Walnuts may be used instead of pecan nuts to make this luxurious and moist teabread.

Makes one 23 x 13cm/ 9 x 5in loaf
175g/6oz/1 cup chopped stoned (pitted) dates
175ml/6fl oz/¾ cup boiling water
50g/2oz/¼ cup unsalted (sweet) butter, at room temperature
50g/2oz/¼ cup soft dark brown sugar
50g/2oz/¼ cup caster (superfine) sugar
1 egg, at room temperature
165g/5½oz/generous 1¼ cups plain (all-purpose) flour
10ml/2 tsp baking powder
2.5ml/½ tsp salt
4ml/¾ tsp freshly grated nutmeg
75g/3oz/¾ cup coarsely chopped pecan nuts

1 Place the dates in a bowl and pour over the boiling water. Set aside to cool. Preheat the oven to 180°C/350°F/Gas 4. Line a 23 x 13cm/9 x 5in loaf tin (pan) with baking parchment and then grease the paper.

2 With an electric mixer, cream the butter and sugars until light and fluffy. Beat in the egg, then set aside.

3 Sift the flour, baking powder, salt and nutmeg together, at least three times. Fold the dry ingredients into the sugar mixture in three batches, alternating with the dates and water. Fold in the chopped pecan nuts.

4 Pour the mixture into the prepared tin and bake until a skewer inserted in the centre comes out clean, about 45–50 minutes.

5 Leave the loaf to cool in the tin for 10 minutes before transferring it to a wire rack to cool completely.

Cook's Tip
To make an adult version of this teabread, you could add 30ml/2 tbsp brandy in step 2, along with the beaten egg.

Energy 2356kcal/9885kJ; Fat 110.3g, Saturated fat 45.4g; Carbohydrate 317g; Fibre 12.4g;

Energy 2458kcal/10331kJ; Fat 101.7g, Saturated fat 32.4g; Carbohydrate 356.4g; Fibre 15.6g

Blueberry Teabread

A lovely crumbly topping with a hint of cinnamon makes this teabread extra special.

Makes 8 pieces

50g/2oz/¼ cup butter or margarine, at room temperature
175g/6oz/scant 1 cup caster (superfine) sugar
1 egg, at room temperature
120ml/4fl oz/½ cup milk
225g/8oz/2 cups plain (all-purpose) flour
10ml/2 tsp baking powder
2.5ml/½ tsp salt
275g/10oz/2½ cups fresh blueberries or bilberries

For the topping

115g/4oz/generous ½ cup caster (superfine) sugar
40g/1½oz/⅓ cup plain (all-purpose) flour
2.5ml/½ tsp ground cinnamon
50g/2oz/¼ cup butter, cut into pieces

1 Preheat the oven to 190°C/375°F/Gas 5. Grease a 23cm/9in baking dish.

2 With an electric mixer, cream the butter or margarine with the caster sugar until light and fluffy. Add the egg and beat to combine, then mix in the milk until well blended.

3 Sift over the flour, baking powder and salt, and stir the mixture just enough to blend the ingredients. Add the blueberries and stir gently. Transfer the teabread mixture to the prepared baking dish.

4 To make the topping, place the caster sugar, flour, ground cinnamon and butter in a mixing bowl. Cut the butter into the dry ingredients using a pastry blender until the mixture resembles coarse breadcrumbs. Sprinkle the topping over the mixture in the baking dish. Bake until a skewer inserted in the centre comes out clean, about 45 minutes. Serve warm or cold.

Variation

In late summer and early autumn, when blackberries are plentiful, try to gather some to use instead of blueberries for this delicious teabread.

Energy 374kcal/1575kJ; Fat 11.7g, Saturated fat 6.9g; Carbohydrate 66.2g; Fibre 2.1g

Dried Fruit Loaf

Use any combination of dried fruit you like in this delicious teabread. The fruit is soaked first making the loaf superbly moist.

Makes one 23 x 13cm/ 9 x 5in loaf

450g/1lb/2¾ cups mixed dried fruit, such as currants, raisins, chopped ready-to-eat dried apricots and dried cherries
300ml/½ pint/1¼ cups cold strong tea
200g/7oz/scant 1 cup soft dark brown sugar
grated rind and juice of 1 small orange
grated rind and juice of 1 lemon
1 egg, lightly beaten
200g/7oz/1¾ cups plain (all-purpose) flour
15ml/1 tbsp baking powder
1.5ml/¼ tsp salt

1 In a bowl, mix the dried fruit with the cold tea and leave to soak overnight.

2 Preheat the oven to 180°C/350°F/Gas 4. Line the base and sides of a 23 x 13cm/9 x 5in loaf tin (pan) with baking parchment and grease the paper.

3 Strain the soaked fruit, reserving the liquid. In a bowl, combine the dark brown sugar, orange and lemon rind, and strained fruit.

4 Pour the orange and lemon juice into a measuring jug (cup); if the quantity is less than 250ml/8fl oz/1 cup, then top up with the soaking liquid.

5 Stir the citrus juices and lightly beaten egg into the dried fruit mixture until combined.

6 Sift the flour, baking powder and salt together into another bowl. Stir the dry ingredients into the fruit mixture until well blended.

7 Transfer to the tin and bake until a skewer inserted in the centre comes out clean: about 1¼ hours. Leave in the tin for 10 minutes before unmoulding.

Energy 2763kcal/11770kJ; Fat 10g, Saturated fat 2g; Carbohydrate 673.9g; Fibre 14.8g

Courgette Teabread

Like carrots, courgettes are a vegetable that works well in baking, adding moistness and lightness to the bread.

Makes one 23 x 13cm/ 9 x 5in loaf
50g/2oz/¼ cup butter
3 eggs
250ml/8fl oz/1 cup vegetable oil
285g/10½oz/1½ cups caster (superfine) sugar

2 unpeeled courgettes (zucchini), grated
275g/10oz/2½ cups plain (all-purpose) flour
10ml/2 tsp bicarbonate of soda (baking soda)
5ml/1 tsp baking powder
5ml/1 tsp salt
5ml/1 tsp ground cinnamon
5ml/1 tsp freshly grated nutmeg
1.5ml/¼ tsp ground cloves
115g/4oz/1 cup chopped walnuts

1 Preheat the oven to 180°C/350°F/Gas 4. Line the base and sides of a 23 x 13cm/9 x 5in loaf tin (pan) with baking parchment and grease the paper.

2 In a pan, melt the butter over a low heat. Set aside.

3 With an electric mixer, beat the eggs and oil together until thick. Beat in the sugar, then stir in the melted butter and the grated courgettes. Set aside.

4 In another bowl, sift the flour with the bicarbonate of soda, baking powder, salt, ground cinnamon, grated nutmeg and ground cloves. Sift twice more and then carefully fold them into the courgette mixture. Fold in the chopped walnuts.

5 Pour into the tin and bake until a skewer inserted in the centre comes out clean, about 60–70 minutes. Leave to stand for 10 minutes before turning out on to a wire rack to cool.

Cook's Tip
Sifting the flour and dry ingredients three times helps to make the teabread mixture light. Be careful to fold in the other ingredients gently so that the air that was incorporated is not lost.

Mango Teabread

This delicious teabread is baked with juicy ripe mango.

Makes two 23 x 13cm/ 9 x 5in loaves
275g/10oz/2½ cups plain (all-purpose) flour
10ml/2 tsp bicarbonate of soda (baking soda)
10ml/2 tsp ground cinnamon
2.5ml/½ tsp salt

115g/4oz/½ cup margarine
3 eggs, at room temperature
285g/10½oz/1½ cups caster (superfine) sugar
120ml/4fl oz/½ cup vegetable oil
1 large ripe mango, peeled and chopped
85g/3¼oz/generous 1 cup desiccated (dry unsweetened shredded) coconut
65g/2½oz/½ cup raisins

1 Preheat the oven to 180°C/350°F/Gas 4. Line the base and sides of two 23 x 13cm/9 x 5in loaf tins (pans) with baking parchment and grease the paper.

2 Sift together the flour, bicarbonate of soda, cinnamon and salt.

3 Cream the margarine until soft. Beat in the eggs and sugar until light and fluffy. Beat in the oil.

4 Fold the dry ingredients into the creamed ingredients in three batches, then fold in the mango, two-thirds of the coconut and the raisins.

5 Spoon the batter into the tins. Sprinkle over the remaining coconut. Bake until a skewer inserted in the centre comes out clean, about 50–60 minutes. Leave to stand for 10 minutes before turning out on to a wire rack to cool completely.

Cook's Tip
A simple way of dicing a mango is to take two thick slices from either side of the large flat stone without peeling the fruit. Make criss-cross cuts in the flesh on each slice and then turn inside out. The cubes of flesh will stand proud of the skin and can be easily cut off.

Fruit and Brazil Nut Teabread

Mashed bananas are a classic ingredient in teabreads, and help to create a moist texture as well as adding a full flavour.

Makes one 23 x 13cm/ 9 x 5in loaf

225g/8oz/2 cups plain
  (all-purpose) flour
10ml/2 tsp baking powder
5ml/1 tsp mixed (apple
  pie) spice
115g/4oz/½ cup butter,
  diced
115g/4oz/½ cup light soft
  brown sugar
2 eggs, lightly beaten
30ml/2 tbsp milk
2 bananas
115g/4oz/⅔ cup dried
  figs, chopped
50g/2oz/⅓ cup brazil
  nuts, chopped

For the decoration
8 whole brazil nuts
4 whole dried figs, halved
30ml/2 tbsp apricot jam

1 Preheat the oven to 180°C/350°F/Gas 4. Grease and base-line a 23 x 13cm/9 x 5in loaf tin (pan). Sift the flour, baking powder and mixed spice into a bowl.

2 Rub in the butter using your fingertips or a pastry cutter until the mixture resembles fine breadcrumbs. Stir in the sugar.

3 Make a well in the centre and work in the eggs and milk until combined. Peel and mash the bananas. Stir in the mashed bananas, chopped figs and brazil nuts and transfer to the prepared loaf tin.

4 To decorate the teabread press the whole brazil nuts and halved figs gently into the mixture, to form an attractive pattern. Bake for 1¼ hours, or until a skewer inserted in the centre comes out clean. Cool in the tin for 10 minutes, then transfer to a wire rack.

5 Heat the jam in a small pan. Increase the heat and boil for 1 minute. Remove from the heat and pass through a fine sieve. Cool the glaze slightly, brush over the warm loaf, and leave to cool completely.

Energy 3095kcal/12984kJ; Fat 145.6g, Saturated fat 72.2g; Carbohydrate 405.9g; Fibre 19.9g

Glazed Banana Spiced Loaf

The lemony glaze perfectly sets off the warm flavours of nutmeg and cloves in this moist banana teabread.

Makes one 23 x 13cm/ 9 x 5in loaf

115g/4oz/½ cup butter,
  at room temperature
165g/5½oz/¾ cup caster
  (superfine) sugar
2 eggs, at room temperature
215g/7½oz/scant 2 cups plain
  (all-purpose) flour
5ml/1 tsp salt
5ml/1 tsp bicarbonate of soda
  (baking soda)
2.5ml/½ tsp freshly
  grated nutmeg
1.5ml/¼ tsp mixed (apple pie)
  spice
1.5ml/¼ tsp ground cloves
175ml/6fl oz/¾ cup sour cream
1 large ripe banana, mashed
5ml/1 tsp vanilla extract

For the glaze
115g/4oz/1 cup icing
  (confectioners') sugar
15–30ml/1–2 tbsp lemon juice

1 Preheat the oven to 180°C/350°F/Gas 4. Line a 23 x 13cm/ 9 x 5in loaf tin (pan) with baking parchment and grease the paper.

2 Cream the butter and sugar until light and fluffy. Add the eggs, one at a time, beating well after each addition.

3 Sift together the flour, salt, bicarbonate of soda, nutmeg, mixed spice and cloves. Add to the butter mixture and stir to combine well.

4 Add the sour cream, banana and vanilla extract, and mix to just blend. Pour this mixture into the prepared tin.

5 Bake until the top springs back when touched lightly, about 45–50 minutes. Cool in the tin for 10 minutes. Turn out on to a wire rack.

6 To make the glaze, combine the icing sugar and lemon juice until smooth, then stir until smooth. Place the cooled loaf on a rack set over a baking sheet. Pour the glaze over the loaf and allow to set.

Energy 3293kcal/13836kJ; Fat 143.6g, Saturated fat 85.4g; Carbohydrate 490.2g; Fibre 7.8g

Banana and Pecan Muffins

These satisfying muffins are quick and easy to make and contain the winning combination of banana and pecan nuts.

Makes 8
150g/5oz/1¼ cups plain (all-purpose) flour
7.5ml/1½ tsp baking powder
50g/2oz/¼ cup butter or margarine, at room temperature
150g/5oz/¾ cup caster (superfine) sugar
1 egg
5ml/1tsp vanilla extract
3 bananas, mashed
50g/2oz/½ cup chopped pecan nuts
75ml/5 tbsp milk

1 Preheat the oven to 190°C/375°F/Gas 5. Lightly grease eight deep muffin cups. Sift the flour and baking powder into a small bowl. Set aside.

2 With an electric mixer, cream the butter or margarine and sugar together. Add the egg and vanilla extract and beat until fluffy. Mix in the banana.

3 Add the pecan nuts. With the mixer on low speed, beat in the flour mixture alternately with the milk.

4 Spoon the mixture into the prepared muffin cups, filling them about two-thirds full. Bake the muffins until golden brown and a skewer inserted into the centre of a muffin comes out clean, about 20–25 minutes.

5 Let the muffins cool in the cups on a wire rack for about 10 minutes. To loosen, run a knife gently around each muffin and unmould on to the wire rack.

6 Leave to cool for another 10 minutes before serving.

Variation
Walnuts also taste good with bananas, so try these instead of pecan nuts for a change.

Energy 277kcal/1164kJ; Fat 10.7g, Saturated fat 4g; Carbohydrate 43.7g; Fibre 1.3g

Blueberry and Cinnamon Muffins

These moist and "moreish" muffins have great appeal.

Makes 8
115g/4oz/1 cup plain (all-purpose) flour
15ml/1 tbsp baking powder
pinch of salt
65g/2½oz/generous ¼ cup soft light brown sugar
1 egg
175ml/6fl oz/¾ cup milk
45ml/3 tbsp vegetable oil
10ml/2 tsp ground cinnamon
115g/4oz/1 cup fresh or thawed frozen blueberries

1 Preheat the oven to 190°C/375°F/Gas 5. Lightly grease eight deep muffin cups.

2 Beat the first eight ingredients together until smooth. Fold in the blueberries. Spoon into the muffin cups, filling them two-thirds full. Bake for 25 minutes, or until lightly coloured. Leave in the cups for 5 minutes then transfer to a rack to cool.

Chocolate-chip Muffins

Makes 10
115g/4oz/½ cup butter or margarine, softened
75g/3oz/⅓ cup granulated sugar
30ml/2 tbsp soft dark brown sugar
2 eggs
175g/6oz/1½ cups plain (all-purpose) flour, sifted twice
5ml/1 tsp baking powder
120ml/4fl oz/½ cup milk
175g/6oz/1 cup plain (semisweet) chocolate chips

1 Preheat the oven to 190°C/375°F/Gas 5. Grease ten muffin cups. Cream the butter or margarine with both sugars until fluffy.

2 Add the eggs, one at a time, beating well after each addition. Fold in the flour, alternating with the milk. Divide half the mixture among the muffin cups. Sprinkle the chocolate chips on top, then cover with the remaining mixture.

3 Bake for 25 minutes. Leave in the tin (pan) for 5 minutes then transfer to a rack to cool.

Top: Energy 141kcal/593kJ; Fat 5.4g, Saturated fat 0.9g; Carbohydrate 21.4g; Fibre 0.9g
Above: Energy 296kcal/1238kJ; Fat 15.8g, Saturated fat 3.4g; Carbohydrate 36.4g; Fibre 1g

Carrot Buns

Using carrots gives these buns a lovely moist consistency, and a delightful taste too.

Makes 12

175g/6oz/3/4 cup margarine, at room temperature
90g/3 1/2oz/generous 1/2 cup soft dark brown sugar
1 egg, at room temperature
15ml/1 tbsp water
225g/8oz/1 1/2 cups grated carrots
150g/5oz/1 1/4 cups plain (all-purpose) flour
5ml/1 tsp baking powder
2.5ml/1/2 tsp bicarbonate of soda (baking soda)
5ml/1 tsp ground cinnamon
1.5ml/1/4 tsp freshly grated nutmeg
2.5ml/1/2 tsp salt

1 Preheat the oven to 180°C/350°F/Gas 4. Grease 12 bun-tray cups or use paper cases.

2 With an electric mixer, cream the margarine and sugar until light and fluffy. Beat in the egg and water, then stir in the grated carrots.

3 Sift over the flour, baking powder, bicarbonate of soda, cinnamon, nutmeg and salt. Stir to blend.

4 Spoon the mixture into the prepared bun tray, filling the cups almost to the top. Bake until the tops spring back when touched lightly, about 35 minutes.

5 Leave the buns to stand for about 10 minutes in the bun tray before transferring to a wire rack to cool completely.

Variation
These mini carrot cakes taste great with a traditional cream cheese topping. Beat 225g/8oz/2 cups icing (confectioners') sugar with 60g/2 1/4oz/generous 4 tbsp cream cheese and 30g/1 1/4oz/generous 2 tbsp softened butter. Add 5ml/1 tsp grated orange rind and blend well. Spread over the tops of the cooked and cooled buns.

Energy 193kcal/803kJ; Fat 12.6g, Saturated gat 0.2g; Carbohydrate 19.2g; Fibre 0.8g

Dried Cherry Buns

Looking for something different? Then try these super little buns with their jewel-like cherries baked inside.

Makes 16

250ml/8fl oz/1 cup natural (plain) yogurt
175g/6oz/3/4 cup dried cherries
115g/4oz/1/2 cup butter, at room temperature
175g/6oz/generous 3/4 cup caster (superfine) sugar
2 eggs, at room temperature
5ml/1 tsp vanilla extract
200g/7oz/1 3/4 cups plain (all-purpose) flour
10ml/2 tsp baking powder
5ml/1 tsp bicarbonate of soda (baking soda)
1.5ml/1/4 tsp salt

1 In a mixing bowl, combine the yogurt and cherries. Cover and leave to stand for 30 minutes. Preheat the oven to 180°C/350°F/Gas 4. Grease 16 bun-tray cups or use paper cases.

2 With an electric mixer, cream the butter and sugar together until light and fluffy. Add the eggs, one at a time, beating well after each addition. Add the vanilla extract and the cherry mixture and stir to blend. Set aside.

3 In another bowl, sift together the flour, baking powder, bicarbonate of soda and salt. Fold into the cherry mixture in three batches.

4 Fill the prepared cups two-thirds full. For even baking, half-fill any empty cups with water. Bake until the tops spring back when touched lightly, about 20 minutes. Transfer to a wire rack to cool completely.

Cook's Tip
If you haven't tried dried cherries before, here is the recipe to begin enjoying their special flavour. They are quite unlike glacé (candied) cherries in that they have a wonderful tart taste. The best variety, Montmorency, has a sweet–sour flavour, perfect for this recipe. Dried cherries also make a healthy snack.

Energy 187kcal/787kJ; Fat 7g, Saturated fat 4g; Carbohydrate 29.9g; Fibre 0.6g

Chelsea Buns

A traditional English recipe, not surprisingly Chelsea buns enjoy wide popularity elsewhere in the world.

Makes 12

225g/8oz/2 cups strong white bread flour
2.5ml/½ tsp salt
40g/1½oz/3 tbsp unsalted (sweet) butter
7.5ml/1½ tsp easy-blend (rapid-rise) dried yeast
120ml/4fl oz/½ cup milk
1 egg, beaten
75g/3oz/½ cup mixed dried fruit
25g/1oz/2½ tbsp chopped mixed (candied) peel
50g/2oz/¼ cup soft light brown sugar
clear honey, to glaze

1 Preheat the oven to 190°C/375°F/Gas 5. Grease a 20cm/8in round tin (pan). Sift together the flour and salt; rub in 25g/1oz/2 tbsp of the butter.

2 Stir in the yeast and make a central well. Slowly add the milk and egg, stirring, then beat until the dough leaves the sides of the bowl clean.

3 Knead the dough for several minutes until smooth. Place in an oiled bowl, cover with oiled clear film (plastic wrap) and set aside until doubled in size.

4 Transfer the dough to a floured surface, gently knock back (punch down) and roll it out to a rectangle 30 x 23cm/12 x 9in.

5 Mix together the dried fruit, peel and sugar in a bowl. Melt the remaining butter and brush over the dough. Sprinkle over the fruit mixture, leaving a 2.5cm/1in border. Roll up the dough from a long side. Seal the edges, then cut into 12 slices.

6 Place the slices, cut sides up, in the greased tin. Cover with clear film and set aside until doubled in size.

7 Bake for 30 minutes, or until a rich golden brown. Brush with honey and leave to cool slightly in the tin before turning out.

Energy 138kcal/582kJ; Fat 3.7g, Saturated fat 2g; Carbohydrate 25g; Fibre 0.8g

Sticky Nut Buns

These tasty buns will be extremely popular with adults and children alike, so save time by making double the quantity and freezing half for another occasion.

Makes 12

160ml/5½fl oz/generous ⅔ cup lukewarm milk
15ml/1 tbsp active dried yeast
30ml/2 tbsp caster (superfine) sugar
450g/1lb/4 cups strong white bread flour
5ml/1 tsp salt
115g/4oz/½ cup cold butter, cut into small pieces
2 eggs, lightly beaten
finely grated rind of 1 lemon

For the filling
275g/10oz/scant 1½ cups soft dark brown sugar
65g/2½oz/5 tbsp butter
120ml/4fl oz/½ cup water
75g/3oz/¾ cup chopped pecan nuts or walnuts
45ml/3 tbsp caster (superfine) sugar
10ml/2 tsp ground cinnamon
165g/5½oz/generous 1 cup raisins

1 Preheat the oven to 180°C/350°F/Gas 4. Mix the milk, yeast and sugar, and leave until frothy. Combine the flour and salt, and rub in the butter. Add the yeast mixture, eggs and lemon rind.

2 Stir to a rough dough. Knead until smooth, then return to the bowl, cover and leave until doubled in size.

3 To make the filling cook the brown sugar, butter and water in a heavy pan until syrupy, about 10 minutes. Place 15ml/1 tbsp syrup in the base of twelve 4cm/½in muffin cups. Sprinkle a thin layer of nuts in each, reserving the remainder.

4 Knock back (punch down) the dough and roll out to a 45 x 30cm/18 x 12in rectangle. Combine the sugar, cinnamon, raisins and reserved nuts. Sprinkle over the dough. Roll up tightly from a long edge and cut into 2.5cm/1in rounds. Place in the muffin cups, cut sides up. Leave to rise for 30 minutes.

5 Bake until golden, about 25 minutes. Invert the tins on to a baking sheet, leave for 5 minutes, then remove the tins. Cool on a wire rack, sticky sides up.

Energy 439kcal/1844kJ; Fat 18.4g, Saturated fat 8.6g; Carbohydrate 66.3g; Fibre 1.7g

Oatmeal Buttermilk Muffins

These easy-to-make muffins make a good alternative to the rich cakes that are so popular at parties.

Makes 12

75g/3oz/scant 1 cup rolled oats
250ml/8fl oz/1 cup buttermilk
115g/4oz/½ cup butter,
    at room temperature
75g/3oz/scant ½ cup soft dark
    brown sugar
1 egg, at room temperature
115g/4oz/1 cup plain
    (all-purpose) flour
5ml/1 tsp baking powder
1.5ml/¼ tsp bicarbonate of soda
    (baking soda)
1.5ml/¼ tsp salt
25g/1oz/¼ cup raisins

1 In a bowl, combine the oats and buttermilk, and leave to soak for 1 hour.

2 Grease 12 muffin cups or use paper cases.

3 Preheat the oven to 200°C/400°F/Gas 6. With an electric mixer, cream the butter and sugar until light and fluffy. Beat in the egg.

4 In another bowl, sift together the flour, baking powder, bicarbonate of soda, and salt. Stir into the butter mixture, alternating with the oat mixture. Fold in the raisins. Take care not to overmix.

5 Fill the prepared cups two-thirds full. Bake until a skewer inserted in the centre comes out clean, 20–25 minutes. Transfer to a rack to cool.

> **Cook's Tips**
> • *For perfect muffins every time never overbeat the batter. Just mix enough to blend, but don't worry about there being a few lumps. An overbeaten batter will result in tough and rubbery muffins.*
> • *If you are not using a tray with muffin cups, use two paper cases for each muffin, to support the batter and stop the sides from collapsing.*

Pumpkin Muffins

Molasses adds a delicious flavour to these spicy muffins. For a change, add chopped dried apricots instead of currants.

Makes 14

150g/5oz/10 tbsp butter or
    margarine, at room temperature
175g/6oz/¾ cup soft dark
    brown sugar
115g/4oz/⅓ cup molasses
1 egg, at room temperature, beaten
225g/8oz/1 cup cooked or
    canned pumpkin
200g/7oz/1¾ cups plain
    (all-purpose) flour
1.5ml/¼ tsp salt
5ml/1 tsp bicarbonate of soda
    (baking soda)
10ml/1 tsp ground cinnamon
5ml/1 tsp freshly grated nutmeg
50g/2oz/¼ cup currants
    or raisins

1 Preheat the oven to 200°C/400°F/Gas 6. Grease 14 muffin cups or use paper cases.

2 With an electric mixer, cream the butter or margarine. Add the sugar and molasses, and beat until light and fluffy.

3 Add the egg and pumpkin and stir until well blended.

4 Sift over the flour, salt, bicarbonate of soda, cinnamon, and nutmeg. Fold just enough to blend; do not overmix.

5 Fold in the currants or raisins.

6 Spoon the batter into the prepared muffin cups, filling them three-quarters full.

7 Bake for 12–15 minutes, or until the tops spring back when touched lightly. Serve warm or cold.

> **Cook's Tip**
> *Strong-flavoured molasses, sometimes called black treacle, is the residue left when cane sugar is refined. Blackstrap molasses, especially, contains small amounts of minerals including iron.*

Energy 172kcal/721kJ; Fat 9.1g, Saturated fat 5.2g; Carbohydrate 20.9g; Fibre 0.8g

Energy 216kcal/906kJ; Fat 9.4g, Saturated fat 5.7g; Carbohydrate 32.5g; Fibre 0.7g

Blueberry Muffins

Hot blueberry muffins with a hint of vanilla are a traditional favourite in the United States.

Makes 12
350g/12oz/3 cups plain
 (all-purpose) flour
10ml/2 tsp baking powder
1.5ml/¼ tsp salt
115g/4oz/½ cup caster
 (superfine) sugar
2 eggs, beaten
300ml/½ pint/1¼ cups milk
115g/4oz/½ cup butter, melted
5ml/1 tsp vanilla extract
175g/6oz/1½ cups
 fresh blueberries

1 Preheat the oven to 200°C/400°F/Gas 6. Grease 12 muffin cups or use paper cases.

2 Sift the flour, baking powder and salt into a large mixing bowl and stir in the sugar.

3 Place the eggs, milk, butter and vanilla extract in a separate bowl and whisk together well.

4 Fold the egg mixture into the dry ingredients with a metal spoon, then gently stir in the blueberries.

5 Spoon the mixture into the muffin cups, filling them to just below the top.

6 Place in the oven and bake for 20–25 minutes, or until the muffins are well risen and lightly browned.

7 Leave the muffins in the cups for about 5 minutes, and then turn them out on to a wire rack to cool. Serve warm or cold.

Variation
Most fruit muffin recipes can be varied to use all kinds of different berries. Try blackcurrants or redcurrants instead of the blueberries here, if you like. Remember to stir the fruit in very gently so that the juice does not "bleed" into the batter.

Apple and Cranberry Muffins with Walnuts

Not too sweet but good and spicy, these muffins will be a favourite with family and friends.

Makes 12
50g/2oz/¼ cup butter
1 egg
90g/3½oz/½ cup caster
 (superfine) sugar
grated rind of 1 orange
120ml/4fl oz/½ cup fresh
 orange juice
150g/5oz/1¼ cups plain
 (all-purpose) flour
5ml/1 tsp baking powder
2.5ml/½ tsp bicarbonate of soda
 (baking soda)
5ml/1 tsp ground cinnamon
2.5ml/½ tsp freshly grated nutmeg
2.5ml/½ tsp mixed (apple
 pie) spice
1.5ml/¼ tsp ground ginger
1.5ml/¼ tsp salt
1 or 2 eating apples
175g/6oz/1½ cups cranberries
50g/2oz/½ cup chopped walnuts
icing (confectioners') sugar,
 for dusting (optional)

1 Preheat the oven to 180°C/350°F/Gas 4. Grease 12 muffin cups or use paper cases. Melt the butter over a gentle heat. Set aside to cool.

2 Place the egg in a mixing bowl and whisk lightly. Add the melted butter and whisk to combine, then add the sugar, orange rind and juice. Whisk to blend.

3 In a large bowl, sift together the flour, baking powder, bicarbonate of soda, spices and salt.

4 Quarter, core and peel the apples. Use a sharp knife to chop them coarsely.

5 Make a well in the dry ingredients and pour in the egg mixture. With a spoon, stir until just blended. Add the apples, cranberries and walnuts, and stir to blend.

6 Fill the cups three-quarters full and bake until the the tops spring back when touched lightly, about 25–30 minutes. Transfer to a wire rack to cool. Dust with icing sugar before serving, if you like.

Scones

Traditionally, scones should be served warm from the oven, with butter, clotted or whipped cream, and jam.

Makes 10–12
225g/8oz/2 cups plain (all-purpose) flour

15ml/1 tbsp baking powder
50g/2oz/4 tbsp cold butter, diced
1 egg, beaten
75ml/5 tbsp milk
1 beaten egg, to glaze

1 Preheat the oven to 220°C/425°F/Gas 7. Lightly butter a baking sheet. Sift the flour and baking powder together, then rub in the butter using your fingertips or a pastry cutter.

2 Make a well in the centre of the flour mixture, add the egg and milk and mix to a soft dough using a round-bladed knife.

3 Turn out the scone dough on to a floured surface, and knead very lightly until smooth.

4 Roll out the dough to about a 2cm/¾ in thickness and cut into ten or twelve circles using a 5cm/2in plain or fluted cutter dipped in flour.

5 Transfer to the baking sheet, brush with egg, then bake for about 8 minutes, or until risen and golden. Cool slightly on a wire rack before serving.

> **Cook's Tips**
> • *For perfectly delicate scones every time, handle the dough as little as possible.*
> • *Always have the oven preheated so that once the dough is made and cut into rounds the scones can go straight into the oven.*
> • *As well as served warm from the oven, scones taste delicious when cool, and are even tasty the next day split and toasted under a preheated grill (broiler). Butter them while they are still hot.*

Drop Scones

If you place the cooked scones in a folded dish towel they will stay soft and moist.

Makes 8–10
115g/4oz/1 cup plain (all-purpose) flour

5ml/1 tsp bicarbonate of soda (baking soda)
5ml/1 tsp cream of tartar
25g/1oz/2 tbsp cold butter, diced
1 egg, beaten
150ml/¼ pint/⅔ cup milk

1 Lightly grease a cast-iron griddle or heavy frying pan, then preheat it.

2 Sift the dry ingredients together, then rub in the butter until the mixture resembles breadcrumbs.

3 Make a well in the centre, then, using a wooden spoon, beat in the egg and sufficient milk to give the mixture the consistency of double (heavy) cream.

4 Drop spoonfuls of the mixture, spaced slightly apart, on to the griddle or frying pan. Cook over a steady heat for 2–3 minutes, until bubbles rise to the surface and burst.

5 Using a metal spatula, turn the scones over and cook for a further 2–3 minutes, or until golden underneath. Serve warm with butter and honey.

> **Cook's Tip**
> *For best results always cook these traditional scones on a cast-iron griddle. The correct heat is important, as the crust of the drop scones will brown too quickly leaving the centre uncooked if the griddle is too hot. If the griddle is too cool, the scones will take too long to cook and will not be as light. To test the heat, preheat the griddle and then sprinkle a little flour over the surface. If it turns golden in about 3 minutes it is ready for the drop scones.*

Energy 104kcal/437kJ; Fat 4.2g, Saturated fat 2.4g; Carbohydrate 14.9g; Fibre 0.6g

Energy 72kcal/303kJ; Fat 3g, Saturated fat 1.6g; Carbohydrate 9.7g; Fibre 0.4g

Orange and Raisin Scones

As well as warm from the oven, these scones are also superb split when cool and toasted under a grill. Butter them while still hot.

Makes 16
275g/10oz/2½ cups plain (all-purpose) flour
25ml/1½ tbsp baking powder
60g/2¼oz/generous ¼ cup caster (superfine) sugar
2.5ml/½ tsp salt
65g/2½oz/5 tbsp butter, diced
65g/2½oz/5 tbsp margarine, diced
grated rind of 1 large orange
50g/2oz/scant ½ cup raisins
120ml/4fl oz/½ cup buttermilk
milk, to glaze

1 Preheat the oven to 220°C/425°F/Gas 7. Grease and flour a large baking sheet.

2 Combine the flour with the baking powder, sugar and salt in a large bowl. Add the butter and margarine, and rub in using your fingertips or a pastry cutter until the mixture resembles coarse breadcrumbs.

3 Add the orange rind and raisins. Gradually stir in the buttermilk to form a soft dough.

4 Roll out the dough to about a 2cm/¾in thickness. Stamp out circles with a cookie cutter. Place on the baking sheet and brush the tops with milk.

5 Bake until golden, about 12–15 minutes. Serve hot or warm, with butter, or whipped or clotted cream and jam.

> **Variations**
> *These scones are also good made with chopped dried apricots, dates or prunes instead of the raisins. Try them spread with honey or orange marmalade, or with cream cheese. Children will also enjoy them with chocolate spread.*

Wholemeal Scones

Split these wholesome scones in two with a fork while still warm and spread with butter and home-made jam, if you wish.

Makes 16
175g/6oz/¾ cup cold butter
350g/12oz/3 cups plain (all-purpose) wholemeal (whole-wheat) flour
150g/5oz/1¼ cups plain (all-purpose) flour
30ml/2 tbsp caster (superfine) sugar
2.5ml/½ tsp salt
12.5ml/2½ tsp bicarbonate of soda (baking soda)
2 eggs
175ml/6fl oz/¾ cup buttermilk
35g/1¼oz/¼ cup raisins

1 Preheat the oven to 200°C/400°F/Gas 6. Grease and flour a large baking sheet.

2 Cut the butter into small pieces. Combine the wholemeal and plain flours with the sugar, salt and bicarbonate of soda in a bowl. Add the butter and rub in using your fingertips or a pastry cutter until the mixture resembles coarse breadcrumbs. Set aside.

3 In another bowl, whisk together the eggs and buttermilk. Set aside 30ml/2 tbsp for glazing, then stir the remaining egg mixture into the dry ingredients until it just holds together. Stir in the raisins.

4 Roll out the dough to about 2cm/¾in thickness. Stamp out circles with a cookie cutter. Place on the baking sheet and brush with the reserved egg and buttermilk glaze.

5 Bake until golden, about 12–15 minutes. Allow to cool slightly before serving.

> **Variation**
> *Raisin scones also go particularly well with cheese, so serve them with a mature (sharp) Cheddar, a full-flavoured blue cheese or a creamy soft cheese such as Camembert or Brie.*

Energy 207kcal/869kJ; Fat 10.3g, Saturated fat 6g; Carbohydrate 25.3g; Fibre 2.3g

Energy 145kcal/606kJ; Fat 6.9g, Saturated fat 2.2g; Carbohydrate 19.8g; Fibre 0.6g

Cheese and Chive Scones

Feta cheese is used instead of butter in these delicious savoury scones, which make a tasty alternative to traditional scones.

Makes 9
115g/4oz/1 cup self-raising (self-rising) flour
150g/5oz/1 cup self-raising (self-rising) wholemeal (whole-wheat) flour
2.5ml/½ tsp salt
75g/3oz feta cheese
15ml/1 tbsp chopped fresh chives
150ml/¼ pint/⅔ cup milk, plus extra to glaze
1.5ml/¼ tsp cayenne pepper

1 Preheat the oven to 200°C/400°F/Gas 6. Sift the flours and salt into a large mixing bowl. Add any bran left in the sieve.

2 Crumble the feta cheese and rub it into the dry ingredients until the mixture resembles breadcrumbs. Stir in the chives, then add the milk and mix to a soft dough.

3 Turn the dough out on to a floured surface and lightly knead until smooth. Roll out to a 2cm/¾in thickness and stamp out scones with a 6cm/2½in cookie cutter.

4 Transfer the scones to a non-stick baking sheet. Brush with milk, then sprinkle with the cayenne pepper. Bake for 15 minutes, or until risen and golden. Cool slightly on a wire rack before serving.

> **Variation**
> For Cheddar cheese and mustard scones, add 2.5ml/½ tsp mustard powder to the flours. Dice 50g/2oz/½ cup cold butter, and rub it into the dry ingredients until the mixture resembles breadcrumbs. Stir 50g/2oz/½ cup grated mature (sharp) Cheddar cheese into the mixture, then pour in the milk. Stir gently to make a soft dough. Roll out on a lightly floured surface and cut into triangles. Place on a baking sheet, brush with milk and sprinkle with 25g/1oz/¼ cup cheese. Bake for 15 minutes, or until well risen.

Energy 124kcal/524kJ; Fat 2.5g, Saturated fat 1.4g; Carbohydrate 21.5g; Fibre 1.9g

Sunflower Sultana Scones

Sunflower seeds give these fruit scones an interesting flavour and texture.

Makes 10–12
225g/8oz/2 cups self-raising (self-rising) flour
5ml/1 tsp baking powder
25g/1oz/2 tbsp soft sunflower margarine
30ml/2 tbsp golden caster (superfine) sugar
50g/2oz/⅓ cup sultanas (golden raisins)
30ml/2 tbsp sunflower seeds
150g/5oz/scant ⅔ cup natural (plain) yogurt
about 30–45ml/ 2–3 tbsp skimmed milk

1 Preheat the oven to 230°C/450°F/Gas 8. Lightly oil a baking sheet. Sift the flour and baking powder into a bowl and rub in the margarine evenly.

2 Stir in the sugar, sultanas and half the sunflower seeds, then mix in the yogurt, with just enough milk to make a fairly soft, but not sticky, dough.

3 Roll out on a lightly floured surface to about a 2cm/¾in thickness. Cut into 6cm/2½in flower shapes or rounds with a cookie cutter and lift on to the baking sheet.

4 Brush with milk and sprinkle with the reserved sunflower seeds, then bake for 10–12 minutes, or until well risen and golden brown. Cool the scones on a wire rack. Serve split, spread with jam or low-fat spread.

> **Cook's Tip**
> Sunflower seeds are a wonder food, and a good and tasty way to add nutrients to the diet, especially selenium, which is often lacking. Don't buy too many at one time and source them from a store where they have a quick turnover so that the ones you buy are fresh. As sunflower seeds have a high fat content they don't store well for long periods. Buy small quantities at a time and put them in a sealed container in a cool place – even a refrigerator.

Energy 121kcal/513kJ; Fat 3.3g, Saturated fat 0.6g; Carbohydrate 21.2g; Fibre 0.8g

Genoese Sponge Cake

This light sponge cake has a firm texture due to the addition of butter and is suitable for cutting into layers for gateaux.

Makes I x 20cm/8in round cake

4 eggs
115g/4oz/generous ½ cup caster (superfine) sugar
75g/3oz/6 tbsp unsalted (sweet) butter, melted and cooled slightly

75g/3oz/²/₃ cup plain (all-purpose) flour

For the flavourings

Citrus: 10ml/2 tsp grated orange, lemon or lime rind
Chocolate: 50g/2oz plain (semisweet) chocolate, melted
Coffee: 10ml/2 tsp coffee granules, dissolved in 5ml/1 tsp boiling water

1 Preheat the oven to 180°C/350°F/Gas 4. Base line and grease a 20cm/8in round cake tin (pan).

2 Whisk the eggs and caster sugar together in a heatproof bowl until thoroughly blended.

3 Place the bowl over a pan of simmering water and continue to whisk the mixture until thick and pale.

4 Remove the bowl from the pan and continue to whisk until the mixture is cool and leaves a thick trail on the surface when the beaters are lifted.

5 Pour the butter carefully into the mixture, leaving any sediment behind.

6 Sift the flour over the surface and add your chosen flavouring, if using. Using a plastic spatula, carefully fold the flour, butter and any flavourings into the mixture until smooth and evenly blended.

7 Scrape the mixture into the prepared tin, tilt to level and bake for 30–40 minutes, until firm to the touch and golden. Cool on a wire rack and decorate as you like.

Quick-mix Sponge Cake

Choose either chocolate or lemon flavouring for this light and versatile sponge cake, or leave it plain.

Makes I x 20cm/8in round or ring cake

115g/4oz/1 cup self-raising (self-rising) flour
5ml/1 tsp baking powder
115g/4oz/½ cup soft margarine

115g/4oz/½ cup caster (superfine) sugar
2 eggs

For the flavourings

Chocolate: 15ml/1 tbsp unsweetened cocoa powder blended with 15ml/1 tbsp boiling water
Lemon: 10ml/2 tsp grated lemon rind

1 Preheat the oven to 160°C/325°F/Gas 3. Grease a 20cm/8in round cake tin (pan), line the base with baking parchment and grease the paper.

2 Sift the flour and baking powder into a bowl. Add the margarine, sugar and eggs with the chosen flavourings, if using.

3 Beat with a wooden spoon for 2–3 minutes. The mixture should be pale in colour and slightly glossy.

4 Spoon the mixture into the cake tin and smooth the surface. Bake in the centre of the oven for 30–40 minutes, or until a skewer inserted into the centre of the cake comes out clean. Turn out on to a wire rack, remove the lining paper and leave to cool completely.

Cook's Tips
• *This sponge cake is ideal for a celebration cake that will be simply iced, but do not use it for a cake that needs to be carved into an intricate shape. Madeira cake is best for that purpose.*
• *Always leave any cake to cool completely before decorating it. It is best to leave it overnight in a sealed, airtight container to settle if possible.*

Energy 1504kcal/6260kJ; Fat 110g, Saturated fat 5.3g; Carbohydrate 107.8g; Fibre 6g

Energy 1736kcal/7280kJ; Fat 89.6g, Saturated fat 48.1g; Carbohydrate 212.5g; Fibre 3.2g

Madeira Cake

This cake is not only delicious plain, it also makes an excellent base to decorate with icing.

Serves 6–8

225g/8oz/2 cups plain (all-purpose) flour
5ml/1 tsp baking powder
225g/8oz/1 cup butter or margarine, at room temperature
225g/8oz/generous 1 cup caster (superfine) sugar
grated rind of 1 lemon
5ml/1 tsp vanilla extract
4 eggs

1 Preheat the oven to 160°C/325°F/Gas 3. Base line and grease a 20cm/8in cake tin (pan).

2 Sift the plain flour and baking powder into a bowl.

3 Cream the butter or margarine, adding the caster sugar about 30ml/2 tbsp at a time, until light and fluffy. Stir in the lemon rind and vanilla extract. Add the eggs one at a time, beating for 1 minute after each addition. Add the flour mixture and stir until just combined.

4 Pour the cake mixture into the prepared tin and tap lightly to level. Bake for about 1¼ hours, or until a metal skewer inserted in the centre comes out clean.

5 Cool in the tin on a wire rack for 10 minutes, then turn the cake out on to a wire rack and leave to cool completely.

Cook's Tips
• *Madeira cake is ideal for using as a celebration cake as it keeps better than a sponge cake and so will last for longer while you decorate it. It also has a firm texture that will be easy to ice with butter icing and sugarpaste.*
• *Level the domed top before icing the cake by putting a deep cake board inside the cake tin (pan) the cake was baked in and placing the cake on top. Cut the part of the cake that extends above the top of the tin using a sharp knife.*

Energy 453kcal/1894kJ; Fat 26.3g, Saturated fat 15.5g; Carbohydrate 51.4g; Fibre 0.9g

Sponge Roll

Vary the flavour of the roll by adding a little grated orange, lime or lemon rind to the mixture, if you like.

Serves 6–8

4 eggs, separated
115g/4oz/½ cup caster (superfine) sugar, plus extra for sprinkling
115g/4oz/1 cup plain (all-purpose) flour
5ml/1 tsp baking powder

For a chocolate flavouring
Replace 25ml/1½ tbsp of the flour with 25ml/1½ tbsp unsweetened cocoa powder

1 Preheat the oven to 180°C/350°F/Gas 4. Base line and grease a 33 × 23cm/13 × 9in Swiss roll tin (jelly roll pan).

2 Whisk the egg whites until stiff peaks form and then beat in 30ml/2 tbsp of the caster sugar.

3 Beat the egg yolks with the remaining caster sugar and 15ml/1 tbsp water for about 2 minutes, or until the mixture is pale and leaves a thick ribbon trail.

4 Sift together the flour and baking powder into another bowl. Carefully fold the beaten egg yolks into the egg whites, then fold in the flour mixture.

5 Pour the mixture into the prepared tin and gently smooth the surface with a plastic spatula.

6 Bake in the centre of the oven for 12–15 minutes, or until the cake starts to come away from the edges of the tin.

7 Turn the cake out on to a piece of baking parchment lightly sprinkled with caster sugar. Peel off the lining paper and cut off any crisp edges.

8 Spread with jam, if you like, and roll up, using the baking parchment to help you.

9 Leave to cool on a wire rack, then dust with icing sugar.

Energy 142kcal/603kJ; Fat 3g, Saturated fat 0.8g; Carbohydrate 26.2g; Fibre 0.5g

Rich Fruit Cake

This is an ideal recipe for a celebration cake. Make this cake a few weeks before icing, wrap and store in an airtight container to mature.

Makes 1 x 20cm/8in round or 18cm/7in square cake

375g/13oz/1½ cups currants
250g/9oz/1½ cups sultanas
  (golden raisins)
150g/5oz/1 cup raisins
90g/3½oz/scant ½ cup glacé
  (candied) cherries, halved
90g/3½oz/generous ½ cup
  almonds, chopped
65g/2½oz/scant ½ cup mixed
  (candied) peel
grated rind of 1 lemon
40ml/2½ tbsp brandy
250g/9oz/2¼ cups plain
  (all-purpose) flour, sifted
6.5ml/1¼ tsp mixed (apple
  pie) spice
2.5ml/½ tsp freshly
  grated nutmeg
65g/2½oz/generous ½ cup
  ground almonds
200g/7oz/scant 1 cup soft
  margarine or butter
225g/8oz/1¼ cups soft light
  brown sugar
15ml/1 tbsp black treacle
  (molasses)
5 eggs, beaten

1 Preheat the oven to 140°C/275°F/Gas 1. Grease a deep 20cm/8in round or 18cm/7in square cake tin (pan), line the base and sides with a double thickness of baking parchment and grease the paper.

2 Combine the ingredients in a large mixing bowl. Beat with a wooden spoon for 5 minutes, or until well mixed.

3 Spoon the mixture into the prepared cake tin. Make a slight depression in the centre.

4 Bake in the centre of the oven for 3–3½ hours. Test the cake after 3 hours. If it is ready it will feel firm and a skewer inserted into the centre will come out clean. Cover the top loosely with foil if it starts to brown too quickly.

5 Leave the cake to cool completely in the tin. Then turn out. The lining paper can be left on until you are ready to ice or serve, to help keep the cake moist.

Light Fruit Cake

This slightly less dense fruit cake is still ideal for marzipanning and icing.

Makes 1 x 20cm/8in round or 18cm/7in square cake

225g/8oz/1 cup soft margarine or
  butter
225g/8oz/generous 1 cup caster
  (superfine) sugar
grated rind of 1 orange
5 eggs, beaten
300g/11oz/2⅔ cups plain
  (all-purpose) flour
2.5ml/½ tsp baking powder
10ml/2 tsp mixed (apple pie) spice
175g/6oz/¾ cup currants
175g/6oz/generous 1 cup raisins
175g/6oz/1 cup sultanas
  (golden raisins)
50g/2oz/¼ cup dried,
  ready-to-eat apricots
115g/4oz/⅔ cup mixed
  (candied) peel

1 Preheat the oven to 150°C/300°F/Gas 2. Grease a deep 20cm/8in round or 18cm/7in square cake tin (pan), line the base and sides with a double thickness of baking parchment and grease the paper.

2 Beat the margarine and sugar together in a large bowl until soft. Add the orange rind and then the eggs, one at a time, beating after each addition and adding a spoonful of flour to stop them curdling. Sift the remaining flour with the baking powder and mixed spice. Stir in the currants, raisins and sultanas.

3 Cut up the apricots in strips, using kitchen scissors, and add to the mixture. Beat thoroughly with a wooden spoon for 3–4 minutes, until thoroughly mixed.

4 Spoon the mixture into the cake tin. Make a slight depression in the centre. Bake in the centre of the oven for 2½–3¼ hours. Test the cake after 2½ hours. If it is ready it will feel firm and a skewer inserted into the centre will come out clean. Test at intervals if necessary. Cover the top loosely with foil if it starts to brown too quickly.

5 Leave the cake to cool completely in the tin, then turn out. The lining paper can be left on until you are ready to ice or serve, to help keep the cake moist.

Energy 7388kcal/31049kJ; Fat 320.2g, Saturated fat 124.8g; Carbohydrate 1047.9g; Fibre 39.1g

Energy 5719kcal/24077kJ; Fat 218.7g, Saturated fat 8.5g; Carbohydrate 918.1g; Fibre 28.3g

Marzipan Roses

To decorate a cake, shape the roses in a variety of colours and sizes then arrange on top.

1 Form a small ball of coloured marzipan into a cone shape. This forms the central core which supports the petals.

2 Take a piece of marzipan about the size of a large pea, and make a petal shape that is thicker at the base.

3 Wrap the petal around the cone, pressing the petal to the cone to secure. Bend back the ends of the petal to curl. Repeat with more petals, each overlapping. Make some petals bigger until the required size is achieved.

Marzipan

Marzipan can be used on its own, under an icing or for modelling decorations.

Makes 450g/1lb/3 cups
225g/8oz/2 cups ground almonds
115g/4oz/generous ½ cup caster (superfine) sugar
115g/4oz/1 cup icing (confectioners') sugar, sifted
5ml/1 tsp lemon juice
a few drops of almond extract
1 egg or 1 egg white

1 Stir the ground almonds and sugars together in a bowl until evenly mixed. Make a well in the centre and add the lemon juice, almond extract and enough egg or egg white to mix to a soft but firm dough, using a wooden spoon.

2 Form the marzipan into a ball. Lightly dust a surface with icing sugar and knead the marzipan until smooth. Wrap in clear film (plastic wrap) or store in a plastic bag until needed. Tint with food colouring if required.

Sugarpaste Icing

Sugarpaste icing is wonderfully pliable and can be coloured, moulded and shaped in imaginative ways.

Makes 350g/12oz/2¼ cups
1 egg white
15ml/1 tbsp liquid glucose, warmed
350g/12oz/3 cups icing (confectioners') sugar, sifted

1 Put the egg white and glucose in a mixing bowl. Stir them together to break up the egg white.

2 Add the icing sugar and mix together with a metal spatula, using a chopping action, until well blended and the icing begins to bind together.

3 Knead the mixture with your fingers until it forms a ball.

4 Knead the sugarpaste on a work surface that has been lightly dusted with icing sugar for several minutes until it is smooth, soft and pliable.

5 If the icing is too soft, knead in some more sifted sugar until it reaches the right consistency.

Cook's Tips
• *Sugarpaste icing is sometimes known as rolled fondant and is available ready made in sugarcraft stores. It is easy to make yourself but if you are using a large quantity and are in a hurry you could purchase it ready made. It is available in a variety of colours.*
• *If you want to make the sugarpaste in advance wrap it up tightly in a plastic bag. The icing will keep for about three weeks.*
• *The paste is easy to colour with paste colours; add a little at a time using the tip of a knife.*
• *Roll out sugarpaste on a surface lightly sprinkled with icing (confectioners') sugar or a little white vegetable fat (shortening) to avoid the paste sticking.*

Energy 2357kcal/9874kJ; Fat 131.1g, Saturated fat 11.5g; Carbohydrate 255.9g; Fibre 16.6g

Energy 1435kcal/6123kJ; Fat 0g, Saturated fat 0g; Carbohydrate 377.6g; Fibre 0g

Royal Icing

Royal icing gives a professional finish. This recipe makes enough icing to cover the top and sides of an 18cm/7in cake.

Makes 675g/1½lb/4½ cups
3 egg whites
about 675g/1½lb/6 cups
  icing (confectioners')
  sugar, sifted
7.5ml/1½ tsp glycerine
a few drops of lemon juice
food colouring (optional)

1 Put the egg whites in a bowl and stir lightly with a fork to break them up.

2 Add the sifted icing sugar gradually, beating well with a wooden spoon after each addition.

3 Add enough icing sugar to make a smooth, shiny icing that has the consistency of very stiff meringue.

4 Beat in the glycerine, lemon juice and food colouring, if using.

5 Leave for 1 hour before using, covered with damp clear film (plastic wrap), then stir to burst any air bubbles.

Cook's Tips
• *The icing will keep for up to three days in a refrigerator, stored in a plastic container with a tight-fitting lid.*
• *This recipe is for an "icing" consistency suitable for flat-icing a marzipanned rich fruit cake. When the spoon is lifted, the icing should form a sharp point, with a slight curve at the end, known as "soft peak". For piping, the icing needs to be slightly stiffer. It should form a fine sharp peak when the spoon is lifted.*
• *Royal icing is not appropriate for a sponge cake, as its stiff consistency would easily drag on the surface.*
• *Never use royal icing direct on to the cake's surface; a layer of marzipan will make a smooth surface for icing and stop cake crumbs mixing with the icing.*

Butter Icing

The creamy rich flavour and silky smoothness of butter icing is popular with both children and adults.

Makes 350g/12oz/1½ cups
75g/3oz/6 tbsp soft margarine or
  butter, softened
225g/8oz/2 cups icing
  (confectioners') sugar, sifted
5ml/1 tsp vanilla extract
10–15ml/2–3 tsp milk

For the flavourings
Chocolate: blend 15ml/1 tbsp
  unsweetened cocoa powder with
  15ml/1 tbsp hot water. Cool
before beating into the icing.
Coffee: blend 10ml/2 tsp coffee
  powder with 15ml/1 tbsp
  boiling water. Omit the milk.
  Cool before beating the mixture
  into the icing.

Lemon, orange or lime: substitute
  the vanilla extract and milk
  with lemon, orange or lime juice
  and 10ml/2 tsp of finely grated
  citrus rind. Omit the rind if
  using the icing for piping.
  Lightly tint the icing with food
  colouring, if you like.

1 Put the margarine or butter, icing sugar, vanilla extract and 5ml/1 tsp of the milk in a bowl.

2 Beat with a wooden spoon or an electric mixer, adding sufficient extra milk to give a light, smooth and fluffy consistency. For flavoured butter icing, follow the instructions above for the flavour of your choice.

Cook's Tips
• *The icing will keep for up to three days in an airtight container stored in a refrigerator.*
• *Butter icing can be coloured with paste colours. Add a little at a time using a cocktail stick (toothpick) until you reach the desired shade.*
• *You can apply butter icing with a knife and make a smooth finish, or you can pipe the icing on to your cake using a plain or fluted nozzle, or use a serrated scraper for a ridged finish.*

Energy 2694kcal/11494kJ; Fat 0g, Saturated fat 0g; Carbohydrate 705.4g; Fibre 0g

Energy 1461kcal/6149kJ; Fat 62g, Saturated fat 0.5g; Carbohydrate 238g; Fibre 0g

Fudge Frosting

A darkly delicious frosting, this can transform a simple sponge cake into one worthy of a very special occasion.

Makes 350g/12oz/1½ cups
50g/2oz plain
   (semisweet) chocolate
225g/8oz icing (confectioners')
   sugar, sifted
50g/2oz/4 tbsp butter
45ml/3 tbsp milk or single
   (light) cream
5ml/1 tsp vanilla extract

1 Break or chop the chocolate into small pieces. Put the chocolate, icing sugar, butter, milk or cream and vanilla extract in a heavy pan.

2 Stir over a very low heat until both the chocolate and the butter have melted. Remove the mixture from the heat and stir until it is evenly blended.

3 Beat the icing frequently as it cools until it thickens sufficiently to use for spreading or piping.

4 Use the icing immediately and work as quickly as possible once it has reached the right consistency. If you let it cool too much it will become too thick to work with.

Cook's Tips
• Spread fudge frosting smoothly over the cake or swirl it. Or be even more elaborate with a little piping – it really is very versatile.
• This recipe makes enough to fill and coat the top and sides of a 20cm/8in or 23cm/9in round sponge cake.
• This icing should be used immediately.
• Use a good quality chocolate so that you achieve a pronounced flavour for this frosting.
• As the frosting contains cream it is best to keep the finished cake in the refrigerator until ready to serve.

Energy 1534kcal/6468kJ; Fat 55.9g, Saturated fat 34.9g; Carbohydrate 269.3g; Fibre 1.3g

Crème au Beurre

The rich, smooth texture of this icing makes it ideal for spreading, filling or piping on to cakes and gateaux.

Makes 350g/12oz/1½ cups
60ml/4 tbsp water
75g/3oz/6 tbsp caster
   (superfine) sugar
2 egg yolks
150g/5oz/10 tbsp unsalted
   (sweet) butter, softened
For the flavourings
Citrus: replace water with orange, lemon or lime juice and 10ml/ 2 tsp grated rind
Chocolate: add 50g/2oz plain (semisweet) chocolate, melted
Coffee: add 10ml/2 tsp instant coffee granules, dissolved in 5ml/1 tsp boiling water, cooled

1 Put the water in a pan and bring to the boil, then stir in the sugar. Heat gently, stirring, until the sugar has dissolved.

2 Boil rapidly until the mixture becomes syrupy, or reaches the "thread" stage (107°C/225°F on a sugar thermometer). To test, place a little syrup on the back of a dry teaspoon. Press a second teaspoon on to the syrup and gently pull apart. The syrup should form a fine thread. If not, return to the heat, boil rapidly and re-test a minute later.

3 Whisk the egg yolks together in a bowl. Continue to whisk while slowly adding the sugar syrup in a thin stream. Whisk until thick, pale and cool. Beat the butter until light and fluffy. Add the egg mixture gradually, beating well after each addition, until thick and fluffy.

4 For Chocolate or Coffee Crème au Beurre, fold in the flavouring at the end.

Cook's Tip
It is important that the syrup reaches the correct stage and does not cook any further, as it will become too firm and you will not be able to whisk it into the egg yolks smoothly.

Energy 1534kcal/6354kJ; Fat 134.3g, Saturated fat 81.3g; Carbohydrate 79.3g; Fibre 0g

American Frosting

A light marshmallow icing which crisps on the outside when left to dry, this versatile frosting may be swirled or peaked into a soft coating.

Makes 350g/12oz/1½ cups
1 egg white
30ml/2 tbsp water
15ml/1 tbsp golden (light corn) syrup
5ml/1 tsp cream of tartar
175g/6oz/1½ cups icing (confectioners') sugar, sifted

1 Place the egg white with the water, golden syrup and cream of tartar in a heatproof bowl. Whisk together until blended.

2 Stir the icing sugar into the mixture and place the bowl over a pan of simmering water. Whisk until the mixture becomes thick and white.

3 Remove the bowl from the pan and continue to whisk the frosting until cool and thick, and the mixture stands up in soft peaks. Use immediately to fill or cover cakes.

Caramel Icing

A rich-tasting icing that makes a lovely cake topping.

Makes 450g/1lb/2 cups
75ml/5 tbsp creamy milk

75g/3oz/6 tbsp butter
30 ml/2 tbsp caster (superfine) sugar
350g/12oz/3 cups icing (confectioners') sugar

1 Warm the milk and butter in a pan. Heat the caster sugar in another pan over medium heat until it turns golden. Immediately remove from the heat before the caramel darkens.

2 Pour the milk mixture over the caramel and return the pan to a low heat. Heat the mixture until the caramel has dissolved, stirring occasionally. Sift in the icing sugar a little at a time, and beat with a wooden spoon until the icing is smooth. Use immediately.

Glacé Icing

An instant icing for quickly finishing the tops of large or small cakes.

Makes 350g/12oz/1½ cup
225g/8oz/2 cups icing (confectioners') sugar
30–45ml/2–3 tbsp hot water
food colouring (optional)

For the flavourings
Citrus: replace the water with orange, lemon or lime juice
Chocolate: sift 10ml/2 tsp unsweetened cocoa powder with the icing (confectioners') sugar
Coffee: replace the water with strong, liquid coffee

1 Sift the icing sugar into a bowl. Using a wooden spoon, gradually stir in enough of the hot water to obtain the consistency of thick cream.

2 Beat until white and smooth, and the icing thickly coats the back of the spoon. Tint with a few drops of food colouring, if you wish, or flavour the icing as suggested above. Use immediately to cover the top of the cake.

Simple Piped Flowers

Bouquets of iced blooms, such as roses, pansies and bright summer flowers, make colourful cake decorations.

Makes 350g/12oz/1½ cup
225g/8oz/2 cups icing (confectioners') sugar
30–45ml/2–3 tbsp hot water

1 For a rose, make a fairly firm icing. Colour the icing. Fit a petal nozzle into a paper piping (icing) bag, half-fill with icing and fold over the top to seal. Hold the piping bag so that the wider end is pointing at what will be the base of the rose and hold a cocktail stick (toothpick) in the other hand.

2 Pipe a small cone shape around the tip of the stick, pipe a petal halfway around the cone, lifting it so that it is at an angle and curling outwards, turning the stick at the same time. Repeat with more overlapping petals. Remove from the stick and leave to dry.

Top: Energy 746kcal/3181kJ; Fat 0g, Saturated fat 0g; Carbohydrate 194.7g; Fibre 0g
Above: Energy 2070kcal/8850kJ; Fat 60.4g, Saturated fat 38.2g; Carbohydrate 404.5g; Fibre 0g

Top: Energy 887kcal/3782kJ; Fat 0g, Saturated fat 0g; Carbohydrate 235.1g; Fibre 0g
Above: Energy 887kcal/3782kJ; Fat 0g, Saturated fat 0g; Carbohydrate 235.1g; Fibre 0g

Honey Icing

A simple and tasty topping for cakes.

Makes 275g/10oz/1¼ cups

75g/3oz/6 tbsp butter, softened
175g/6oz/1½ cups icing
(confectioners') sugar
15ml/1 tbsp clear honey
15ml/1 tbsp lemon juice

1 Put the softened butter into a bowl and gradually sift over the icing sugar, beating well after each addition.

2 Beat in the honey and lemon juice and combine well. Spread over the cake immediately.

Butterscotch Frosting

Soft light brown sugar and treacle make a rich and tempting frosting for cakes.

Makes 675g/1½lb/3 cups
75g/3oz/6 tbsp unsalted
(sweet) butter
45ml/3 tbsp milk
25g/1oz/2 tbsp soft light
brown sugar
15ml/1 tbsp black
treacle (molasses)
350g/12oz/3 cups icing
(confectioners') sugar, sifted

For the flavourings
*Citrus: replace the treacle with
golden (light corn) syrup and
add 10ml/2 tsp finely grated
orange, lemon or lime rind*
*Chocolate: sift 15ml/1 tbsp
unsweetened cocoa
powder with the icing
(confectioners') sugar*
*Coffee: replace the treacle
(molasses) with 15ml/1 tbsp
coffee granules*

1 Place the butter, milk, sugar and treacle in a bowl over a pan of simmering water. Stir until the butter melts and the sugar dissolves completely.

2 Remove from the heat and stir in the icing sugar. Beat until smooth. For different flavourings, follow the instructions above. Pour over the cake, or cool for a thicker consistency.

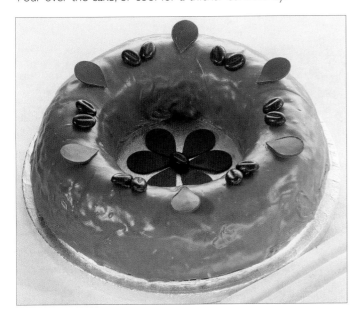

Chocolate Fudge Icing

A rich glossy icing which sets like chocolate fudge, this is versatile enough to smoothly coat, swirl or pipe, depending on the temperature of the icing when it is used.

Makes 450g/1lb/2 cups
115g/4oz plain (semisweet)
chocolate, in squares
50g/2oz/¼ cup unsalted
(sweet) butter
1 egg, beaten
175g/6oz/1½ cups icing
(confectioners')
sugar, sifted

1 Place the chocolate and butter in a heatproof bowl over a pan of hot water.

2 Stir the mixture occasionally with a wooden spoon until both the chocolate and butter are melted. Add the egg and beat well until thoroughly combined.

3 Remove the bowl from the pan and stir in the icing sugar, then beat until smooth and glossy.

4 Pour immediately over the cake for a smooth finish, or leave to cool for a thicker spreading or piping consistency.

Chocolate Curls

These tasty curls look spectacular on a gateau.

Makes around 20 curls
115g/4 oz plain (semisweet)
chocolate

1 Melt the chocolate, then pour on to a smooth surface, such as marble or plastic laminate. Spread evenly over the surface with a palette knife. Leave to cool slightly.

2 Hold a large, sharp knife at a 45° angle to the chocolate and push it along the chocolate in short sawing movements from right to left to make curls. Lift off with the knife and leave to cool.

Top: Energy 1291kcal/5420kJ; Fat 61.6g; Saturated fat 39.1g; Carbohydrate 194.8g; Fibre 0g
Above: Energy 2095kcal/8850kJ; Fat 62.4g; Saturated fat 39.5g; Carbohydrate 404.5g; Fibre 0g

Top: Energy 1722kcal/7235kJ; Fat 78.8g, Saturated fat 46.9g; Carbohydrate 256.2g; Fibre 2.9g
Above: Energy 29kcal/123kJ; Fat 1.6g; Saturated fat 1g; Carbohydrate 3.7g; Fibre 0.1g

Apricot Glaze

It is a good idea to make
a large quantity of apricot
glaze, especially when
making celebration cakes.

Makes 450g/1lb/1½ cups
450g/1lb/generous 1½ cups
apricot jam
45ml/3 tbsp water

1 Place the jam and water in a pan. Heat gently, stirring
occasionally, until the jam has melted.

2 Boil the jam rapidly for 1 minute, then rub through a sieve,
pressing the fruit against the sides of the sieve with the back of
a wooden spoon.

3 Discard the skins left in the sieve.

4 Use the warmed glaze to brush cakes before applying
marzipan, or use for glazing fruits on gateaux and cakes.

Pastillage

This paste sets very hard
and is used for making firm
decorative structures from
icing sugar.

Makes 350g/12oz/1¼ cups
300g/11oz icing
(confectioners') sugar
1 egg white
10ml/2 tsp gum tragacanth

1 In a large bowl, sift most of the icing sugar over the egg
white, a little at a time, stirring continuously until the mixture
sticks together.

2 Add the gum tragacanth and transfer the mixture to a work
surface which has been dusted with icing sugar.

3 Knead the mixture well until the ingredients are thoroughly
combined and the paste has a smooth texture.

4 Knead in the remaining icing sugar and mix until stiff.

Sugar-frosting Flowers

Choose edible flowers such
as pansies, primroses, violets,
roses, freesias, apple
blossom, wild bergamot
(monarda), borage,
carnations, honeysuckle,
jasmine and pot marigolds.

**Makes 10–15 flowers,
depending on their size**
1 egg white
caster (superfine) sugar
10–15 edible flowers

1 Lightly beat an egg white in a small bowl and sprinkle some
caster (superfine) sugar on a plate.

2 Wash the flowers then dry on kitchen paper. Evenly brush
both sides of the petals with the egg white. Hold the flower
by its stem over a plate lined with kitchen paper, sprinkle it
evenly with the sugar, then shake off any excess. Place on a
wire rack covered with kitchen paper and leave to dry in
a warm place.

Glossy Chocolate Icing

A rich smooth glossy icing,
this can be made with plain
or milk chocolate.

Makes 350g/12oz/1¼ cups
175g/6oz plain
(semisweet) chocolate
150ml/¼ pint/⅔ cup single
(light) cream

1 Break up the chocolate into small pieces and place it in a pan
with the cream.

2 Heat gently, stirring occasionally, until the chocolate has
melted and the mixture is smooth.

3 Allow the icing to cool until it is thick enough to coat the
back of a wooden spoon. Use it at this stage for a smooth
glossy icing, or allow it to thicken to obtain an icing which can
be swirled or patterned with a cake decorating scraper.

Top: Energy 1175kcal/5022kJ; Fat 0g, Saturated fat 0g; Carbohydrate 311.9g; Fibre 0g
Above: Energy 1453kcal/6190kJ; Fat 5.5g; Saturated fat 1.6g; Carbohydrate 365.8g; Fibre 0g

Top: Energy 6kcal/24kJ; Fat 0g; Saturated fat 0g; Carbohydrate 1.1g; Fibre 0.1g
Above: Energy 1182kcal/4937kJ; Fat 77.7g, Saturated fat 47.6g; Carbohydrate 114.4g; Fibre 4.4g

Petal Paste

Makes 500g/1¼lb

10ml/2 tsp powdered gelatine
25ml/1½ tbsp cold water
10ml/2 tsp liquid glucose
10ml/2 tsp white vegetable
   fat (shortening)
450g/1lb/4 cups icing
   (confectioners') sugar, sifted
5ml/1 tsp gum tragacanth
1 egg white

1 Place the gelatine, water, liquid glucose and white fat in a heatproof bowl set over a pan of hot water until melted, stirring occasionally.

2 Remove the bowl from the heat.

3 Sift the icing sugar and gum tragacanth into a large bowl. Make a well in the centre and add the egg white and the gelatine mixture.

4 Thoroughly combine the ingredients to form a soft malleable white paste.

5 Knead the paste on a surface dusted with icing sugar until smooth, white and free from cracks.

6 Place in a plastic bag or wrap in clear film (plastic wrap), sealing well to exclude all the air.

7 Leave the paste for about two hours before using, then knead again and use small pieces at a time, leaving the remaining petal paste well sealed.

Piping Twisted Ropes

Fit nozzles nos 43 or 44, or a writing nozzle, into a baking parchment piping (icing) bag and half-fill with royal icing. Hold the bag at a slight angle and pipe in a continuous line with even pressure, twisting the bag as you pipe.

Energy 1888kcal/8044kJ; Fat 8.2g, Saturated fat 3.6g; Carbohydrate 478.3g; Fibre 0g

Marbling

Sugarpaste lends itself to tinting in all shades and marbling is a good way to colour the paste.

1 Using a cocktail stick (toothpick), add a little of the chosen edible food colour to some sugarpaste icing. Do not knead the food colouring fully into the icing.

2 When the sugarpaste is rolled out, the colour is dispersed in such a way that it gives a marbled appearance.

Meringue Frosting

This wonderfully light and delicate frosting needs to be used immediately.

Makes 450g/1lb/1½ cups

2 egg whites
115g/4oz/1 cup icing
   (confectioners') sugar, sifted
150g/5oz/⅔ cup unsalted
   (sweet) butter, softened

For the flavourings

*Citrus: 10ml/2 tsp finely grated
   orange, lemon or lime rind.*
*Chocolate: 50g/2oz plain
   (semisweet) chocolate, melted*
*Coffee: 10ml/2 tsp coffee
   granules, blended with 5ml/
   1 tsp boiling water, cooled*

1 Whisk the egg whites in a clean, heatproof bowl, add the icing sugar and gently whisk to mix well. Place the bowl over a pan of simmering water and whisk until thick and white. Remove the bowl from the pan and continue to whisk until cool when the meringue stands up in soft peaks.

2 Beat the butter in a separate bowl until light and fluffy. Add the meringue gradually, beating well after each addition, until thick and fluffy. Fold in the chosen flavouring, using a metal spatula, until evenly blended. Use immediately for coating, filling and piping on to cakes.

Energy 1592kcal/6620kJ; Fat 123.3g, Saturated fat 78.1g; Carbohydrate 121.1g; Fibre 0g